"Drawing from a rich array of ancient and contemporary sources, Emilio Alvarez takes us on a brief and fascinating journey through various meanings and expressions of Pentecost. Readers will gain a fresh appreciation for this season of the church year."

Christine Pohl, professor emerita of Christian ethics at Asbury Theological Seminary

"Emilio Alvarez's gifting as a thoughtful scholar and caring pastoral practitioner is on full display in his work *Pentecost.* Alvarez was created to craft this book. His deep love and passion for the church are evident throughout the text. Alvarez's study is historically rich, theologically sound, ecumenically inclusive, and prophetically challenging all at the same time. Alvarez helps us to look back, within, and forward in a pilgrimage toward Pentecost."

Charles O. Galbreath, senior pastor of Alliance Tabernacle, Brooklyn, and associate dean at Alliance Theological Seminary

"This volume offers a brilliant reflection on the meaning of the great feast of Pentecost. Alvarez masterfully weaves biblical and historical references to help readers see the powerful light that this feast brings to the world, namely the light of God's manifest presence. Moreover, Alvarez's anointed and beautiful writing creates a hunger for more of the divine light."

Cheryl Bridges Johns, visiting professor and director of the Pentecostal House of Study at United Theological Seminary

Emilio Alvarez

Esau McCaulley, SERIES EDITOR

Pentecost

A Day of Power for All People

Fullness of Time series

An imprint of InterVarsity Press
Downers Grove, Illinois

InterVarsity Press
P.O. Box 1400 | Downers Grove, IL 60515-1426
ivpress.com | email@ivpress.com

Cover design and image composite: David Fassett
Interior design: Daniel van Loon

ISBN 978-1-5140-0054-0 (print) | ISBN 978-1-5140-0055-7 (digital)

Printed in the United States of America ♾

Library of Congress Cataloging-in-Publication Data
Names: Alvarez, Emilio, 1979- author.
Title: Pentecost : a day of power for all people / Emilio Alvarez.
Description: Downers Grove, IL : IVP Books, [2022] | Series: The fullness of time series | Includes bibliographical references.
Identifiers: LCCN 2022048462 (print) | LCCN 2022048463 (ebook) | ISBN 9781514000540 (print) | ISBN 9781514000557 (digital)
Subjects: LCSH: Pentecost season.
Classification: LCC BV61 .A48 2022 (print) | LCC BV61 (ebook) | DDC 252/.64—dc23/eng/20221121
LC record available at https://lccn.loc.gov/2022048462
LC ebook record available at https://lccn.loc.gov/2022048463

29 28 27 26 25 24 23 | 11 10 9 8 7 6 5 4 3 2 1

Contents

The Fullness of Time

SERIES PREFACE

ESAU MCCAULLEY, GENERAL EDITOR

C hristians of all traditions are finding a renewed appreciation for the church year. This is evident in the increased number of churches that mark the seasons in their preaching and teaching. It's evident in the families and small groups looking for ways to recover ancient practices of the Christian faith. This is all very good. To assist in this renewal, we thought Christians might find it beneficial to have an accessible guide to the church year, one that's more than a devotional but less than an academic tome.

The Fullness of Time project aims to do just that. We have put together a series of short books on the seasons and key events of the church year, including Advent,

Christmas, Epiphany, Lent, Easter, and Pentecost. These books are reflections on the moods, themes, rituals, prayers, and Scriptures that mark each season.

These are not, strictly speaking, devotionals. They are theological and spiritual reflections that seek to provide spiritual formation by helping the reader live fully into the practices of each season. We want readers to understand how the church is forming them in the likeness of Christ through the church calendar.

These books are written from the perspective of those who have lived through the seasons many times, and we'll use personal stories and experiences to explain different aspects of the season that are meaningful to us. In what follows, do not look for comments from historians pointing out minutiae. Instead, look for fellow believers and evangelists using the tool of the church year to preach the gospel and point Christians toward discipleship and spiritual formation. We pray that these books will be useful to individuals, families, and churches seeking a deeper walk with Jesus.

The Power of Pentecost

AN INTRODUCTION

But you shall receive power when the Holy
Spirit has come upon you; and you shall be
witnesses to Me in Jerusalem, and in all Judea
and Samaria, and to the end of the earth.

ACTS 1:8 NKJV

B ut you shall receive power."
Imagine being a first-century Jewish fisherman or homemaker in Roman-occupied Judea and hearing these words. Amid the sociopolitical, socioreligious, and socioeconomic upheaval of the times, the promise of power to a first-century Jew would have been greatly appealing. Such conditions were adverse to the freedom, independence, and prosperity promised to the children of Israel in former covenants, and if anything can be said to be true

today in comparison to the time in which the promise was made, it's that people yearn for power.

If, as Esau McCaulley puts it elsewhere in this Fullness of Time series, "Lent is inescapably about repentance," then Pentecost is inescapably about power. So what kind of power dynamics are involved in Pentecost? Does Pentecost promise political or economic power? The New Testament writers use the word *power* in one form or another over 120 times, translated from roughly six different Greek words: *exousia, dynamis, ischys, kratos, energeia,* and *biastēs.*[1] Of these, the two words connected to the coming and abiding presence of the Holy Spirit and its promises are *dynamis* (power) and *exousia* (authority). When Jesus tells his disciples in Acts 1:8 that they would receive power (*dynamis*) when the Holy Spirit came upon them, he was speaking of the inherent power or strength to perform miracles, or to have moral power or excellence of soul.[2] Yet he also speaks to them about the power (*exousia*/authority) that has been given to him (Matthew 28:18), which he in turn gives to his disciples to cast out evil spirits and heal the sick (Matthew 10:1).

Today's contemporary ways of both being in and reflecting on the world usually prevent us from grasping the magnitude of what Jesus' promise of power meant to his disciples, let alone what it means for us today. What was true then is still true now: most people in the world feel powerless. Religious, political, economic, and relational circumstances have us all asking questions: What's going on in the world—or, for that matter, the church? Why is such-and-such happening? What can we (normal everyday believers) do about it?

Today, however, it seems as though believers are more focused on power apart from its pneumatological or christological context and instead have become consumed by presidential power, economic power, or military power. Of course, as human beings in a world of commerce and information technology, we must grapple with these notions, yet it seems we emphasize them over the power that derives from the coming of the Holy Spirit at Pentecost.

Indeed, even in Jesus' day many saw his ministry as a movement of social and political power that would produce change. This is evident in the Gospel of John where the people, after seeing that Jesus has the power to provide sustenance, attempt to make him king by force (John 6:15). To be certain, power does mean having the ability or authority to produce change both personally and in others. As Brigid Harrison, an American academic, author, and professor of political science at Montclair State University, suggests:

> Power is exercised over individuals and groups by offering them things they value or by threatening to deprive them of those things. These values are the base of power, and they can include physical safety, health, and well-being; wealth and material possessions; jobs and means to a livelihood; knowledge and skills; social recognition, status, and prestige; love, affection, and acceptance by others; and a satisfactory self-image and self-respect. To exercise power, then, control must be exercised over the things that are valued in society.[3]

Yet this overemphasis on political, economic, or even religious power has actually led to a sense of powerlessness that affects Christian believers from all backgrounds who continue to deal with denominational divides, theological doubt, spiritual apathy, clerical cynicism, and spiritual fatigue. As if things were not bad enough, the current fad toward the deconstruction of Christianity and its negative effects due to the misuse of power and various kinds of abuse within the church has led many believers toward atheism.[4]

The power we need now is not the power of a certain political branch of government or the promises of power by business leaders. The power we need now is the power of Pentecost, which is intimately connected to the message of the good news of the Christ who lived, died, and was raised, who is proclaimed as gospel in accordance with the Scriptures, who is present in the breaking of the bread, and who is experienced still today by the power of the Holy Spirit.

This power comes not only to us but through us and for us. Just like the first-century Jews living in Roman-occupied Judea, we who live in the here and now suffer the effects of political corruption, financial uncertainty, social injustice, and racial discrimination. And like them, we look for the power to change both our personal lives and the lives of others. Fundamentally, this is what we mean by the Christian celebration of Pentecost.

In spite of the never-ending woes of the world, every year for almost two thousand years Christians of all traditions from all over the world have gathered fifty days after

Easter to commemorate, observe, and celebrate the coming of the Holy Spirit. Pentecost (the Greek word used in the Septuagint, or Greek Old Testament, for "fiftieth") has been known by some Christians as the church's birthday, while for other Christians it speaks of the empowerment of the church by the Holy Spirit in order to accomplish the mission it was given. To be clear, in celebrating Pentecost we do not celebrate the active work of the Holy Spirit as if it were never present. To the contrary, at Pentecost we acknowledge and celebrate that the Spirit who was active at creation, throughout history, and in the ministry of Christ now, as Laurence Stookey suggests, "constitutes the church of God."[5]

There are those who in commemorating Pentecost hold in tension the narrative of Acts 2 as read through the lens of Joel 2:28 with the spiritual phenomenon that occurred in 1906 during the Azusa Street Revival in Los Angeles, the origin of the modern Pentecostal movement. This type of bodily kinesthetic worship involved swaying and dancing as well as the joyful raising and the clapping of hands. For these Pentecostals (in a spiritual or denominational sense), the Azusa Street Revival was a renewal movement that, according to Arthur Wallis, emphasized "the fullness of the Holy Spirit as a distinct experience, and its affirmation that the supernatural gifts of the Holy Spirit bestowed at Pentecost have never been permanently withdrawn from the church."[6] Others in the Christian tradition adopt a more liturgical, ritualistic practice regarding Pentecost, one that includes ancient prayers and Scriptures, which we will also examine within this work.

Interestingly, Pentecost is the oldest season of the church's calendar year, going all the way back to the Jewish feast or festival of seven weeks.[7] It is so called because it was celebrated seven weeks or fifty days after Passover, which now corresponds to Triduum. The actual day of Pentecost celebrates the descent of the Holy Spirit (Acts 2:1-13), the recapitulation (retelling) of the historic promise of the Spirit, the retelling of the great gospel story (Acts 2:14-39), and the growth of the church in the power of the Spirit (Acts 2:40-47).

A fact not readily known is that before the fourth century, Pentecost (as well as Easter and Ascension) were all celebrated together as one Paschal feast.[8] The developments that contributed to Pentecost being celebrated as a standalone feast within the Christian calendar are said to have come from the need for more Christian feasts or holidays over and against pagan feasts.[9] Another surprising fact is that Pentecost is one of three festivals (Passover, Pentecost, and Sukkot) that are considered "Pilgrim Festivals." They are called Pilgrim Festivals because in ancient times, when the temple was in Jerusalem, Jews were required to make pilgrimage to pray at the temple on each of these festivals (Exodus 34:23).

The concept of pilgrimage in general has to do with making a certain journey to a certain sacred place laden with religious meaning. During a pilgrimage the pilgrim concentrates not so much on arriving at their destination as much as the time between when they start their journey and when they arrive.

Journey is a crucial concept for us to understand as we view ourselves as both pilgrims and sojourners during Pentecost. To celebrate Pentecost is to acknowledge that, first and foremost, as believers in Christ, we are strangers and sojourners in the world, holding temporary residence (1 Peter 2:11-12; John 17:14-15), yet just as the Jews traveled to the temple in Jerusalem three times a year, we are also pilgrim believers on a journey. As Hebrews 11:13-14 describes, we are part of our ancestors (Abraham,

Abel, Enoch, Sarah, and Noah), heroes of the faith who died in the faith knowing they were "seeking a homeland." And just as the fathers and mothers of old, as well as the rest of the church triumphant, during Pentecost we include ourselves in the pilgrimage that ultimately leads to our final destination: eternal life in heaven (Matthew 24:13). As Psalm 84 reminds us:

> Blessed *is* the man whose strength *is* in You,
> Whose heart *is* set on pilgrimage.
> *As they* pass through the Valley of Baca,
> They make it a spring;
> The rain also covers it with pools.
> They go from strength to strength;
> *Each one* appears before God in Zion.
>   (Psalm 84:5-7 NKJV)

The season of Pentecost is not only about the promise of spiritual power that aids us in our everyday living but about the power given to us so we might become children of God (John 1:12) and, as children of God, strangers in the world and pilgrims journeying toward our heavenly eternal home. This pilgrimage is not to the temple in Jerusalem but to the temple that lies within, which has not been made by human

hands (Acts 7:48). The pilgrimage that Pentecost's celebration brings to our remembrance is a journey toward our
own hearts. Pentecost is a time (as we will see) where we
take each of the fifty days to travel closer and closer to the
God who dwells in our hearts. We are inspired as Christian
believers to take this journey day by day, equipped with our
own personal experiences, biblical stories and Scriptures,
prayers, and, yes, even symbolic rituals.

Before we move on from the notion of Pentecost as
pilgrimage, I believe it is of ultimate importance that we
decipher whether we are acting as pilgrims or tourists in
our Christian celebration of Pentecost. Peter Bremer, a
teacher and scholar of American religious history, quotes
Professor Peter Brown as saying:

> The difference between pilgrimage and tourism has
> to do with the worthiness of the traveler. Pilgrims . . .
> go on their journeys to make themselves worthy to
> experience *praesentia*, the physical presence of the
> saint. . . . Pilgrims' travels, at least ideally in Christian
> practice, amount to an exercise in humility, dedi-
> cation, and faith.
>
> In contrast, tourists travel with an attitude of en-
> titlement. They enter holy grounds as consumers of

the sacred, rather than as humble souls worthy of the sacred presence.[10]

As Brown notes, the difference between the pilgrim and the tourist has more to do with the inner workings of the heart than the outward action of traveling feet. For the pilgrim, the road traveled is not for the pleasure of sightseeing or consumerist enjoyment but for embracing the suffering and hardship of a difficult road, which becomes the tool of our humility. It is in this act of pilgrimage that we join the countless martyrs of the faith, counting ourselves with them as worthy. As we reflect on Pentecost as journey, we must ask ourselves a question: Are we truly pilgrims willing to endure hardship, suffering, and humility along this deep path toward our own hearts? Or are we tourists looking to be entertained by notions of what's better for me and mine?

Pentecost

A Feast of Fifty Days, First Fruits, and Harvest

*When the Day of Pentecost had fully come, they
were all with one accord in one place.*

Acts 2:1 NKJV

When you hear the word *feast*, what mental images come to mind? I imagine a large celebration filled with close family, dear friends, and tons of good food. To have a feast is to celebrate! And yet this aspect of the celebration of Pentecost often goes unconsidered.

In this chapter I endeavor to explore and examine with you the various feasts with which Pentecost is identified. From a biblical perspective, Pentecost has been known by many names in the Hebrew Old Testament that translate into themes pertinent to our Christian-Judeo spirituality.

A Feast of Fifty Days

The first Hebrew name for Pentecost in the Old Testament is *Hag Hashavuot,* or the Festival of Weeks, *Hag* meaning "feast" or "festival" and *Shavuot* meaning "periods of seven."[1] The Feast of Weeks was celebrated on the "fiftieth day after the ceremony of the waving of the omer of barley, which itself was to take place on the day after the Sabbath after Passover (Leviticus 23:15-16)."[2] This chronological reference specifies the amount of time between Passover and Pentecost. Often so much attention is given to the actual day of Pentecost as narrated in Acts 2, along with the supernatural events surrounding it ("a sound from heaven, as of a rushing mighty wind," and "tongues, as of fire"), that equally if not more important events go unnoticed. I have always asked myself why Luke, the writer of Acts, uses the phrase, "When the day of Pentecost had fully come . . . ," what does "fully come" mean? Also, other than Jesus' command to assemble in Jerusalem, what other reason would there be for Luke to bring to his readers' attention the fact that "they were all with one accord in one place"? This is where the theme of Pentecost as a feast celebration that counts the day by day encourages the reader to focus on and celebrate the fifty days within Pentecost instead of the actual day of Pentecost.

Unlike its two contemporary festivals (Passover and Sukkot), Pentecost as the Feast of Weeks is the only festival where the Israelites were commanded to count the days leading up to the actual feast (Leviticus 23:15-16; Deuteronomy 16:9). In fact, each of the fifty days of Pentecost were not only to be counted but were treated with importance, and were days of rejoicing. For early Christians, "every day was treated in the same way as Sunday, that is, with no kneeling for prayer or fasting," according to Bradshaw and Johnson.[3] This particular focus on honoring or celebrating the fifty days of Pentecost reminds me of the notion of the sanctification of time in Abraham Heschel's work *The Sabbath*:

> While the deities of other peoples were associated with places or things, the God of Israel was the God of events: the Redeemer from slavery, the Revealer of the Torah, manifesting Himself in events of history rather than in things or places. Thus, the faith in the unembodied, in the unimaginable was born. Judaism is a religion of time aiming at the sanctification of time.[4]

This notion of the sanctification of time—especially during periods of uncertainty such as pandemic fatigue, financial stress, religious apathy, and relational struggles—can be found in the counting of days in Pentecost. It reminds us once again of God's sovereignty over the processes of our lives. And it could be one of the reasons Luke was so determined to start his narrative by stating, "When the day of Pentecost had fully come."

If you were to look for the phrase "in the fullness of time" in the New Testament, you would find it only twice. Historically speaking, the first mention is found in Paul's declaration of God sending his Son in Galatians: "But when the fullness of the time had come, God sent forth His Son, born of a woman, born under the law, to redeem those who were under the law, that we might receive the adoption as sons" (Galatians 4:4-5 NKJV). The second instance is found in Acts 2 as discussed above, which speaks of God sending his Spirit and is the text that serves as the main verse for this chapter. The expressions "fullness of time" and "had fully come" actually speak of two specific periods of time, one characterized by preparation and the other by fulfillment. Though different, both periods are interrelated. One of the facts of life is that often we are more preoccupied with the fulfillment of a thing than the preparation for that thing. What would it have meant for those men and women in the upper room to have waited day in and day out for the promise of the Holy Spirit? How did they wait?

A Hebrew name given to Pentecost that is not found in the Old Testament but has rather been historically adopted and falls in line perfectly with the notion of Pentecost as a feast of the fifty days is *Z'Man Mattan Toratenu,* which translates into "the giving of the law."[5] This particular historical designation speaks both to the belief that the Feast of Weeks correlates with the giving of the law at Mount Sinai and also to what the Festival of Weeks became after the temple was destroyed. Here Pentecost became a time for Jews to stay up all night rehearsing the book of Ruth and the giving of the law in Exodus 19–20, as well as the Decalogue or Ten Commandments, as later Jewish tradition described Pentecost.[6]

How are we encouraged by both the Old Testament and New Testament witness of Pentecost to wait on the Lord? Surely we no longer wait for the promise of the Holy Spirit, which has already been fulfilled, but we wait nonetheless for the things in which we believe.

Elisabeth Elliot famously said, "The devil has made it his business to monopolize on three elements: noise, hurry, crowds."[7] Pentecost as a feast of the day by day is a time when we rediscover the joy of waiting on the promises of God by the power of the Holy Spirit. It is a time when we celebrate not only the fulfillment of a promise but also the preparation that moves us toward that promise. It is a time when we intentionally slow down and consider living not in the future to come or the past that was but in the day-to-day present that is.

Interestingly, unlike our modern Christian practice, the early church placed a special emphasis on the fifty days of Pentecost and even utilized biblical imagery to expand its spiritual meaning. While for today's Christian the meaning of Pentecost resides mostly within the day of Pentecost, the early church fathers found prolific spiritual meaning in the symbolism of the fifty days. For example, Clement of Alexandria, one of the earliest Christian theologians, in arguing for the mystical meanings of numbers and geometrical ratios, saw the fifty days of Pentecost as resembling the width of the ark Noah was commanded to make. For Clement, the fifty days of Pentecost, like Noah's Ark, was a "symbol of hope and remission or pardon."[8] This concept of forgiveness and pardon was shared by Origen, another early Christian scholar and a student of Clement.

For Origen, the width of Noah's Ark was a reminder that "according to the law, indeed there was a time for forgiveness of debts every fifty years."[9]

The law Origen makes mention of is the law of jubilee found in Leviticus 25:8-17. There the children of Israel are commanded to set free all slaves and return all property that had been leased or mortgaged to the original owners every fiftieth year (Leviticus 25:10). This theme of forgiveness and pardon, although abundant in the early church's teaching regarding Pentecost, is one the modern church has ignored or has no knowledge of at all. Usually we attribute themes like forgiveness and pardon to seasons like Lent, yet we must not miss its centrality in Pentecost as well. With its focus on fifty days, Pentecost is a season of preparation and fulfillment as well as a season that counts the day to day and gifts us power to forgive as we ourselves have been forgiven.

A FEAST OF THE FIRST FRUITS

The second Hebrew name found in the Old Testament for Pentecost is *Hag Habikkurim,* or the Festival of First Fruits. The Hebrew word *bikkurim* is connected to the root word *bekhor,* which refers to the firstborn. "On the day of the first fruits, when you offer a grain offering of new grain to the LORD at your festival of weeks, you shall have a holy convocation; you shall not work at your occupations" (Numbers 28:26). As a festival of the first fruits, *Hag Habikkurim* required that either the firstborn man or firstborn animal be given to God: "Consecrate to me all the firstborn; whatever is the first to open the womb among the Israelites, of human beings and animals, is mine" (Exodus 13:2). Honoring and obeying the command to dedicate to God the first fruits came with a promise of overflowing barns, vats, and new wine (Proverbs 3:9-10). "Later Tradition mandated that the first fruits be brought only from certain crops known as the 'seven species.' These were the seven products of Israel mentioned in Deuteronomy 8:8: wheat, barley, grapes, figs, pomegranates, olives, and dates (honey dates)."[10]

Speaking of first fruits, I am almost always terrified to hear modern clergy and laity alike refer to first fruits in the context of wealth or prosperity. While there is an economic concept tied to the notion of first fruits, the actual Christian spiritual practice comes not from the offering of natural grain or wheat but from Christ himself. Cyril of Alexandria, a Christian bishop and doctor of the church, in speaking of Pentecost's Old Testament practice of offering the sheaves and first fruits, states that these must now be interpreted in light of the life, passion, death, and resurrection of Christ: "Then contemplate the first-fruits of renewed humanity, that is to say, Christ Himself, in the figure of the sheaf and in the first-fruits of the field and in the first ears of grain, offered in holy oblation to God the Father."[11] Cyril's characterization of Christ as both sheaf and first fruit offered to God leads Jean Daniélou to conclude:

> The feast of the harvest is seen to be the figure of the Resurrection of Christ under the double aspect which characterizes the content of the feast; first it is an offering, and this is a figure of the offering of Christ to His Father, of the sacrificial character of the Resurrection; and secondly, it is an offering of first-fruits; and Christ is Himself the first-fruits of redeemed humanity.[12]

When we think about a reinterpreted Pentecost spirituality in the light of Christ, two major themes should be prominent and celebrated in relation to the concept of first fruits. First, the theme of sacrifice as an offering should remind us that in giving our time, our finances, and even our talents and gifts, we are (to some extent) modeling the sacrificial and resurrected nature of Christ, who paid it all through his own sacrifice (Hebrews 10:11-14) and who rose from the grave, ascended, and presented himself to his Father (John 20:17; Luke 24:51; Acts 1:9-11). Celebrating Christ as our offering (Hebrews 9:28) should be a standard practice in the life of the believer. Yet many times our own sacrificial giving of our lives, talents, and monetary gifts is hampered by regret and suspicion. Pentecost is the feast in which we are reminded that God loves a cheerful first fruit giver.

Second, above and beyond any economic gift or gift of time we might make, nothing can replace the offering of ourselves as a renewed and redeemed humanity (Psalm 107:2; Ephesians 1:7; 4:22-24). As 1 Peter reminds us, in and through Christ we are a chosen generation, a royal priesthood, a holy nation, his own special people, that we may proclaim the praises of him who called us out of darkness into his marvelous light (1 Peter 2:9). Therefore, our first fruit Pentecost offering should be first and foremost that of a redeemed and renewed life in and through Christ, which as a consequence means we have gifts of finances, time, and talents to offer.

A Feast of the Harvest

The third Hebrew name given to Pentecost in the Old Testament is *Hag Hakatsir,* which means the Festival or Feast of Harvest: "You shall observe the festival of harvest, of the first fruits of your labor, of what you sow in the field" (Exodus 23:16). Pentecost celebrated the end of the barley harvest and the beginning of the wheat harvest.[13] Both barley and wheat as grain crops would have been planted together in autumn, yet barley matured quickly while wheat took much more time.[14] In fact, the wheat harvest took up the whole spring, up to mid-May. According to Sejin Park, "The completion of harvest was a natural opportunity for celebration since it signified divine blessing and material abundance, and was a natural point in the agricultural cycle to take a break from work."[15]

In the Gospels, Jesus refers to the harvest when he observes the throngs of people who come to him during his teaching and healing ministry:

When he saw the crowds, he had compassion for them, because they were harassed and helpless, like sheep without a shepherd. Then he said to his disciples, "The harvest is plentiful, but the laborers are few; therefore ask the Lord of the harvest to send out laborers into his harvest." (Matthew 9:36-38)

Imagine this scene. In the Gospels of both Matthew and Luke, Jesus looks out into the multitude and is moved with compassion toward them. Yet he tells his disciples to pray that the Lord of the harvest might send out laborers. I've always asked myself why Jesus didn't tell his disciples *they* were the laborers—to go and reap this harvest now? The answer is that the disciples had not yet been filled with power. And just as those in the natural world had to wait fifty days for the harvest to completely come in, so the disciples had to wait fifty days, not only for the things they had seen and experienced to take root and produce fruit within them, but to be filled with the Spirit.

The difference now is that instead of taking a break to celebrate the end of the hard work, we are sent out in the power of the Spirit to reap the ever-growing and ripening harvest. This is why Pentecost continues to be a harvest feast or celebration, because we celebrate the fact that finally, at Pentecost, the laborers were sent into God's harvest. Hallelujah!

While there are those who are entertained by notions of acknowledging only two sendings in the Christian narrative

(God sending his Son and God sending his Spirit in the filioque), believers need to pay close attention to the Pentecost account, which teaches that there are actually three sendings in the New Testament. At Pentecost, the Holy Spirit is sent by the Father and comes in order that we, those who receive the Spirit, might be sent out into the world (harvest) to make disciples (Matthew 28:19). As the Feast of Harvest reminds us, we are the empowered laborers who look upon a ripe harvest of souls in need of reaping.

2

Learning to Speak in Other Tongues

PENTECOST AND ITS MULTILINGUAL, COMMUNAL SPIRITUALITY

All of them were filled with the Holy Spirit and began to speak in other languages, as the Spirit gave them ability.

ACTS 2:4

I am often asked the question, What does it mean to be biblically Pentecostal? Does someone have to belong to a particular denomination or ascribe to a particular spirituality? Over the years, as I have reflected on the question, the verse noted above in connection to the notion of being multilingual remains at forefront of my thinking.

Historically, speaking in other tongues has been a highly contested practice since its inception. After the close of the New Testament, most of the classical writings are muted at best on the subject. Morton Kelsey in his book *Tongue Speaking* insists that, given all the accusations against early Christians (they were responsible for floods, earthquakes, eating of newborn babies, and so on), the early church writers would have shied away from the topic of tongues in order not to "have added fuel to the fire that flamed into irrational rejection of Christians as monsters."[1]

For Kelsey, Irenaeus's reflection on the conversion of Cornelius's household demonstrates the length the patristic writers went to in order to avoid the topic of tongues. In speaking of Peter's visit to Cornelius in Acts 10, Irenaeus states, "Neither for a like reason, would he [Peter] have given them baptism so readily, had he not heard them prophesying when the Holy Ghost rested upon them."[2] The issue with Irenaeus's comment is that Acts 10:44-46 never uses the word "prophesying" to describe what happened when the Holy Spirit fell on those who heard the gospel, which, in Irenaeus's view, convinced Peter to baptize them. What convinced Peter to baptize Cornelius's household (as the biblical narrative shows) is that Peter and those with him "heard them speaking in tongues and extolling God" (Acts 10:46). Prophesying was never part of the original story, yet Irenaeus felt compelled to switch out "tongues" for "prophesy," probably to avoid some type of ridicule. This type of avoidance continues for the most part throughout classical Christian history, although there are sporadic mentions of interpretation of tongues (Tertullian) and the language of angels (Saint Pachomius).[3]

Given that most of the early church either understood the topic of glossolalia (speaking in tongues) differently or avoided the topic altogether, one can probably understand why the events at the Azusa Street Revival in 1906, with its focus on ecstatic manifestations (including tongues), were seen as a recovery or renewal of the Holy Spirit's outpouring in Acts 2. Yet, while some see this kinesthetic bodily and spiritual action as the basis of their spirituality through an "initial evidence," the action itself as associated with Pentecost in Acts 2 has an even deeper meaning.

UNDOING THE CURSE OF BABEL

Distinct from the gift of speaking in tongues—which edifies only the individual believer and was to be exercised by two or three in the church assembly, each taking their turn, followed by an interpretation of what was said (see 1 Corinthians 14)—the tongues spoken in the upper room at Pentecost were actual languages. Laurence Stookey in his work *Calendar: Christ's Time for the Church* sees Pentecost in Acts 2 as "the undoing of the curse of Babel" found in Genesis 11.[4] At the tower of Babel the whole world had one language and one word, and they did not want to be scattered throughout the earth but rather decided to build a national identity. Notice that they speak one language and one word. Here we see the beginnings of a nationalist way of thinking ("we speak English in this country"), to which God responds by coming down and confusing their tongues.

Pentecost in Acts 2 is a reversal of Genesis 11 in that God does not give everyone the ability to speak one language as much as he empowers humanity to understand each other through other languages. Those in the upper room hear and understand the wonders of God in other languages, which, contrary to Babel, shows us what it means to have a united diverse community of the Spirit. In this community each and every one of the persons represented not only understand each other but understand what God is doing in each other. Babel represents a prideful divisive humanity where confusion, misunderstanding, and misdirection are involved, while Pentecost represents the opposite, as Saint Gregory of Nazianzus's *Oration on Pentecost* makes clear:

> But as the old Confusion of tongues was laudable, when men who were of one language in wickedness and impiety, even as some now venture to be, were building the Tower; for by the confusion of their language the unity of their intention was broken up, and their undertaking destroyed; so much more worthy of praise is the present miraculous one. For being poured from One Spirit upon many men, it brings them again into harmony. And there is a diversity of Gifts, which stands in need of yet another Gift to discern which is the best, where all are praiseworthy.[5]

Pentecost is the anti-Babel event in the life of the Christian church, and as such it contradicts and counteracts any divisive monopoly toward a spirituality lacking immersion into cultural and linguistic diversity. In doing so, Pentecost promotes a multiethnic, multicultural, and multilingual approach to our Christian faith.

In his stellar commentary on 2 Kings 18–19, Walter Brueggemann renarrates the story of the Assyrian army at the gates of Jerusalem attempting to siege Judah. An Assyrian negotiator stands at the city walls and, speaking in Hebrew, demands Judah's surrender. The leaders of Judah, upon hearing the Assyrian negotiator, respond, "Please speak to your servants in the Aramaic language, for we understand it; do not speak to us in the language of Judah within the hearing of the people who are on the wall" (2 Kings 18:26). Brueggemann, in reflecting on the Old Testament narrative, makes a distinction between the "conversation at the wall" being had by Assyrian negotiators with the leaders of Judah and the "conversation behind the wall," which was held in the ordinary language of the people. The Assyrians were purposefully using Hebrew in the conversation at the wall in order to scare any who heard. The leaders of Judah demanded that they speak Aramaic, the language of diplomacy. The conversation behind the wall speaks to the conversation of the everyday person, including King Hezekiah's own conversation with God. Brueggemann's point is that there is an ordinary language for living and another for engagement in diplomacy.

Pentecost displays the power and importance of a Spirit-led multilingual reality that supersedes national linguistic boundaries and even breaches the political. Even the Assyrians who primarily spoke Aramaic had enough sense to know that in order to be a world power, a secondary language was important. The same is true of those empowered by the Spirit of Pentecost. While everyone has a first language of Christian spirituality or faith (be it Roman Catholic, Methodist, Anglican, Pentecostal, or Orthodox), the Spirit on the day of Pentecost propels believers to go beyond their established language of faith into an empowered, multilingual experience of Christian spirituality. Christians who believe in Pentecost as an anti-Babel event should be able to exhibit not only cultural multilingual sensitivity but also an ecumenical and spiritual multilingual ability as well. If we are all one church and indeed the body of Christ, then Pentecost brings us together. It is at Pentecost where I keep my primary language of Pentecostal Christian spirituality but also acknowledge and yearn to learn a second or third language of Christian spirituality and faith.

Living as a Multilingual Community

During the fifty days of Pentecost, what if we were to visit other Christian churches that did not speak our primary language of faith? What if the Pentecostal went to a Roman Catholic Church and vice versa? What if the Anglican went over to an Orthodox Church while the Orthodox believer went over to a Baptist church? Would that not resemble what occurred at the day of Pentecost, where everyone heard each other in their own tongue speaking the wonderful deeds of God? Here's an even more accurate cultural-biblical depiction: What if the White American went to an African American church or a South Asian went to a Korean church or a Latino/a went to a Native American church?

Elsewhere I have designated this kind of intentional, multilingual, ecumenical movement brought on by and through the power of the Holy Spirit at Pentecost as "an ecumenism of the Spirit."[6] This new ecumenism resembles translocal and transnational networks that "follow the flow of markets as they cross not only national boundaries but national languages or tongues as well." Whereas in the old ecumenism one could be and represent only one thing, the new ecumenism is "emergent, convergent, charismatic, pentecostal, missional, evangelical, constructive," and it allows for participation in more than one Christian tradition.[7] It is inclusive of women and people of color as principal players within countermovements that oppose most of the old political ecumenism.[8]

Not only does Pentecost empower us to be culturally and ecclesially multilingual, it also restores the communal sensibility that should be at the forefront of our celebration of Pentecost. Pentecost is communal, not individual, empowerment. Stookey states that Pentecost

> is a crucial means of reinforcing the notion that this day is about the church as the community of the Spirit, not merely about the work of the Spirit in the hearts of individuals. Babel results in disconnectedness, in a confused individualism. The church implies reconnectedness, such as that set forth in Paul's metaphor of the church as a body having many parts. Each different but in need of the others (1 Corinthians 12:4-31).[9]

Here we are reminded of the communal description found in Romans 14:17: "For the kingdom of God is not food and drink but righteousness and peace and joy in the Holy Spirit." While I believe one can have a personal relationship with God, an individual relationship implies the absence of communal relationship. Pentecost also reminds us of the relationship between the Holy Spirit, righteousness, and community, noting that to properly express the kingdom of God within each and every one of us is to exhibit the righteousness, peace, and joy that can come only in the Holy Spirit. All three concepts are communal in nature.

A Restoration of Identity

Another biblical narrative commonly associated with Pentecost and its linguistic and covenantal nature is the event on Mount Sinai described in Exodus. Scholars such as Sejin Park and Raymond E. Brown see Pentecost in Acts 2 as the completion of God's appearance and covenant to Moses and the people of Israel at Sinai. Park states:

> The Ascension and Pentecost narrative draws on the Sinai event and consciously draws a parallel between Moses' ascent of Mt. Sinai during the third month (the month of the Festival of Weeks) and return with the Law, on the one hand, and Jesus'

ascension from Mt. Olivet and the sending of the Spirit during Pentecost at Jerusalem, on the other.[10]

This direct association leads Park to believe that Pentecost as found in Acts 2, similar to the Sinai event in Exodus, brings about a restoration of identity as "the people of God."[11] While the covenant in Exodus is associated with the Ten Commandments, at Pentecost the covenant is intimately connected to the sending of the Holy Spirit.

For Raymond Brown, the event at Pentecost holds in common with the event at Mount Sinai not only the matter of ascension, but a number of descriptive supernatural manifestations as well. He notes:

In depicting God's appearance at Sinai, Exodus 19 includes thunder and smoke; and the Jewish writer Philo (contemporary with the New Testament) describes angels taking what God said to Moses on the mountain top and carrying it out on tongues to the people on the plain below. Acts, with its description of the sound of a mighty wind and tongues as of fire, echoes that imagery, and thus presents the Pentecost in Jerusalem as the renewal of God's covenant, once more calling a people to be God's own.[12]

Brown's recalling of the imagery of tongues as displayed in both Philo's depiction of the event on Mount Sinai and the description of Pentecost in Acts 2 focuses on the covenantal nature of language between God and humankind as well as between humankind and humankind. This aspect of language, culture, and ethnicity within the framework of a covenantal community of the Spirit is precisely the main aspect of Pentecost that so often goes overlooked.

But Pentecost in Acts 2 is not just an invitation to become a covenantal people with God through the metaphor of language (tongues). Our present conversation along with Gregory's oration brings us to a question: Can a church really be Pentecostal or celebrate Pentecost without embracing the concept of a united diverse humanity as a community of the Spirit? If at Pentecost the miracle of a united culture and language transcended all human imagination, shouldn't our local churches at Pentecost reflect the same?

How biblically Pentecostal are we if our church services or ministries (social, educational, developmental, and so on) are conducted in only one language? Furthermore, in celebrating Pentecost, can we honestly be content with concentrating on metaphors and imagery of fire, thunder, and wind, which conjure up ecstatic emotions during worship, without ever focusing on the social, cultural, and linguistic dynamics of Pentecost as exhibited in Acts 2? Pentecost, as we have examined, is not only about the ability to be bilingual or trilingual in your proclamation or hearing of the gospel; it is also about our ability to hear others "speaking in our own tongues the wonderful works of God" (Acts 2:11 NKJV). Here Pentecost calls us to embody a crosscultural recognition of God's work in the life of the "other."

Can a White North American Christian recognize and understand what God is doing in the life of an African American Christian? Can an African American Christian recognize and understand what God is doing in the life of a White North American Christian? Can both White and Black Christians recognize and understand what God is doing in Latin Americans, Asians, and other ethnicities and cultures represented in our global cities? Here lies the transformative power of Pentecost. Can we at Pentecost intentionally include people from other cultures and languages in our celebrations and reflections in order to hear the wonders of God through their lives? Here and in these actions the Holy Spirit prepares humanity to be together at the end of all things:

After this I looked, and there was a great multitude that no one could count, from every nation, from all tribes and peoples and languages, standing before the throne and before the Lamb, robed in white, with palm branches in their hands. They cried out in a loud voice, saying,

"Salvation belongs to our God who is seated on the throne, and to the Lamb!" (Revelation 7:9-10)

3

How Shall We Move?

RITUALS OF PENTECOST

After you've done all you can
After you've gone through the hurt
After you've gone through the pain . . .
Prayed and cried . . .
After you've done all you can, you just stand.

DONNIE MCCLURKIN

Rituals connected to Pentecost vary depending on the Christian tradition. Pentecost itself usually falls on a different date for Eastern and Western Christians due to the fact that most Western churches follow the Gregorian calendar while Eastern Orthodox churches usually follow the Julian calendar. Beyond the date itself, however, a number of varied traditions throughout the church universal reflect the rich symbolism of the coming of the Holy Spirit and the worship that event has evoked through the ages.

THE COLORS OF PENTECOST

Another difference in how Pentecost is celebrated between Western and Eastern churches is in the liturgical colors and decorations used to mark the season. For example, most Western churches use either white or red in their liturgical decorations and dress (both for clergy and people) as symbolic markers of Pentecost. The use of white calls to mind another term used to identify Pentecost: Whitsunday. According to the *Oxford Dictionary of the Christian Church*, Whitsunday is "the feast of the descent of the Holy Spirit upon the Apostles on the 50th day after Easter."[1] Whitsunday (Pentecost) became the second-most preferred date for baptisms after Easter, thus the name "Whitsunday" was derived from "the white robes worn by the newly baptized on that day."[2] The white robe was a sign of the new believer's transformation by grace through baptism,[3] but it also symbolized the eschatological hope that looks forward to the end of all things, as we see in Revelation 7:9: "There was a great multitude . . . standing before the throne and before the Lamb, robed in white."

Today the multitude of Christians who wear white for Pentecost probably do so without understanding this eschatological context. For some, the color white may have more to do with the symbolic dove that rested on Jesus and thus also came upon those gathered in the upper room. But historically and biblically, the color white goes beyond that. When we wear white for Pentecost, we first acknowledge and reaffirm our transformation through baptism by the power of the Spirit. Second, we acknowledge and look to the future hope of the second coming of our Lord Jesus Christ, who grants us eternal life.

This theme of life everlasting at Pentecost is attributed to the earliest Christian thinkers, particularly Saint Athanasius, who in his reflections states, "When a certain number of days have gone by, we shall celebrate the solemnity of holy Pentecost, whose cycle of days is a figure of the future world in which, living always with Christ, we shall praise the God of the universe."[4] Whitsunday is still celebrated as such by some in the Northwest region of the Church of England (Anglican Church), where parades called "whit walks" still take place.[5]

Somewhere along the line in the West, the focus on baptism and white robes on the day of Pentecost transitioned to an emphasis on the presence and work of the Holy Spirit, and therefore the color red was adopted to symbolize the Spirit as flames of fire that rested on the heads of the disciples. Red as a liturgical color prompts us to consider not only the various symbolisms associated with the metaphor of fire (purification, warmth, passion, and so on), but within the church it also causes us to consider passion, God's love, and Christ's blood shed on the cross, as well as the celebration of the Christian martyrs.[6] Red also continues the symbolism derived from Revelation 7:13 where the white robes of the saints have been washed in the blood of the Lamb:

> Then one of the elders addressed me, saying, "Who are these, robed in white, and where have they come from?" I said to him, "Sir, you are the one that knows." Then he said to me, "These are they who have come out of the great ordeal; they have washed their robes and made them white in the blood of the Lamb.
>
> For this reason they are before the throne of God,
>   and worship him day and night within his temple,
>   and the one who is seated on the throne will shelter them." (Revelation 7:13-15)

Contrary to the Western use of red, Eastern Orthodox churches mainly use the color green for Pentecost. Churches are decorated with greenery and flowers and Orthodox clergy wear green vestments. For Orthodox Christians, the color green at Pentecost symbolizes life, particularly the life the Holy Spirit breathes into the hearts of believers.[7] It also follows the tradition of the Jewish holiday Shavuot, which celebrates the giving of the Mosaic law. In addition, the color green at Pentecost is connected to the *semik* (Slavic) or *rusalki* (Russian), an ancient festival "closely linked with the cult of the dead and the spring agricultural rites. It usually fell upon the Thursday of the Green Week (better known as Trinity Week in Russia and the Whitsuntide week in Great Britain)."[8]

STANDING IN THE SPIRIT

Another Pentecost ritual is the prohibition of kneeling for prayers during the fifty days of Pentecost. In early church practice, Sunday was connected to the resurrection of Jesus (on the third day) and was a day of rejoicing and celebration; therefore no kneeling was permitted in order that believers would embody a more upright, positive posture.[9] Standing is a common posture for prayer in the

Bible: "Whenever you stand praying, forgive, if you have anything against anyone; so that your Father in heaven may also forgive you your trespasses" (Mark 11:25). This practice is also found as early as Tertullian (AD 155–220), who states, "We count fasting or kneeling in worship on the Lord's Day to be unlawful. We rejoice in the same privilege also from Easter to Whitsunday (Pentecost)."[10] The same prohibition is also found and upheld by the ecumenical Council of Nicaea (AD 325). In an effort "to see that certain points of liturgical discipline judged important be universally observed,"[11] the twentieth canon reads, "Seeing that certain people kneel on Sunday and during the Pentecost season, so that there might be the same practice in all the communities, it has been decided by the holy council that prayers should be addressed to the Lord standing up."[12] Finally, Saint Basil the Great (AD 329–379) provides possibly the best reasoning for the prohibition of kneeling on Sundays and beyond:

> In the same way, during all the fifty days after Pascha (Easter) we are reminded of the anticipated resurrection. . . . During this time, the customs and orientation of the Church have taught us to prefer the standing position in prayer, thus transposing

our minds from the present to the future by this outward physical reminder.[13]

As Saint Basil suggests, the practice of standing for prayer, particularly during the fifty days of Pentecost, is a physical reminder that helps prepare us for the second coming of the Lord. Standing can also be a posture of resistance against the world through the power of the same Spirit that resurrected Christ from the dead (Romans 8:11). As the old adage usually attributed to Alexander Hamilton says, "If you don't stand for something, you'll fall for anything." This could have been what Paul was thinking when he admonished the church of Ephesus to "take up the whole armor of God, so that you may be able to withstand on that evil day, and having done everything, to stand firm" (Ephesians 6:13) or he encouraged the church in Galatia to "stand fast therefore in the liberty by which Christ has made us free, and do not be entangled again with a yoke of bondage" (Galatians 5:1 NKJV).

At Pentecost, we stand in prayer in order that we might demonstrate our steadfastness and faith in God and the work he is doing in, through, and for us. This does not necessarily mean all is well. In fact, as you read these very words, you might be struggling to recover the power you've lost in finances, in relationships, or within your own self, and yet Pentecost is a season of bold declarations and bold postures where we learn, as the famous songwriter Donnie McClurkin declares, that after we've done all we can, we "just stand!"

KNEELING IN HUMILITY

> Your love brings me to my knees . . .
> You are all my heart desires.
> Until the end of time
> My soul surrendered.[14]

After a period of fifty days of standing for prayer, Pentecost concludes with what are known as the "kneeling prayers." Kneeling for prayer is also a common biblical custom. While the posture of standing in prayer represents resistance as well as future eschatological hope, joy, and confidence, kneeling in prayer expresses humility and penitence.[15] Luke, the writer of Acts, describes how Paul, after he had admonished the Ephesian elders, "knelt down with them all and prayed" (Acts 20:36). While kneeling has recently also taken on a designation of resistance or awareness, in the biblical and spiritual sense it is an act of humility and worship before God (2 Chronicles 7:3; Psalm 95:6; Philippians 2:9-11).

The Greek word that best demonstrates this type of kneeling is *proskynein* or *proskynēsis,* which speaks of "a common gesture of supplication or reverence. The physical act ranged from full prostration to a genuflection, a bow, or a simple greeting."[16] Kneeling can also be an outward showing of repentance or pleading, as in the account of the man who has an epileptic son in Matthew 17:14-21. In fact, there are many examples of people kneeling before Jesus (Greek word *gonypetein*) and asking him to heal them of one sickness or another (Mark 1:40; 10:17). There is even an example of Roman soldiers kneeling in mockery as Jesus made his way toward crucifixion (Matthew 27:29).

4

Pentecost Prayers, Hymns, and Scriptures

There is a treasure trove of Scripture readings, prayers, and hymns for Pentecost stored within the history of the one holy, catholic, and apostolic church. Each tradition's libraries are replete with their own liturgical prayer books or missals outlining and guiding their adherents toward the proper celebration of the seasons within the liturgical calendar. Given the volume of liturgical resources for Pentecost available for each Christian tradition, I won't deal with every tradition directly. Instead, I will present a particular sampling of liturgical materials in hopes of providing new formational resources for celebrating Pentecost. The Christian traditions we will discuss in this chapter are Eastern Orthodox, Roman Catholic, Syrian Orthodox, Anglican, and Pentecostal.

EASTERN ORTHODOX

The Eastern Orthodox tradition is rich with Scriptures, prayers, and hymns that exalt the role and presence of the Holy Spirit. That there are continuing ecstatic movements of the Spirit within Eastern Orthodoxy is a fact that cannot be denied and that invites Christian believers of all traditions to explore further. In particular, the tradition's monastic history features both men and women who have written of their ecstatic experiences with the Holy Spirit. One of these is Saint Symeon the New Theologian in the eleventh century. Symeon shares the designation "new theologian" with only two other saints, John the Evangelist and Gregory of Nazianzus. He is called "new theologian" mainly because he was the first to experience the ecstatic light of the Spirit and call it God. An example of one of Symeon's spiritual visions of divine light is captured in his twenty-fifth hymn, which for the purpose of this subject on Pentecost I have included here at length:

> Master, I saw your face, how shall I describe it?
> I looked upon your beauty, how shall I speak of
>   what is unspeakable. . . .

I was sitting in the light of a lamp.
Its light shone on me, it lit up the darkness
and the shadow of night.
I was reading in the light of the lamp,
reflecting on words, examining statements.

Then, Master, as I was meditating on these things,
suddenly you appeared from above,
much larger than the sun.
As a ray of brilliant light you shone from heaven
        into my heart.

Everything else I saw as shadow.
Except that in the middle there was a column
of light that cut through the air
passing from heaven down to me. . . .

At once I forgot the light of the lamp.
I was no longer aware of being inside the house.
I seemed to sit surrounded by darkness.
I lost contact with my body.
But I said to you and I say it again from the
bottom of my heart:
"Have mercy on me, Master
 have mercy on me, my all. . . . "

But oh what intoxication of light,
oh what movements of fire!
Oh what swirlings of the flame in me coming
from you and your glory!
And all this in spite of my nothingness!

I recognize the glory.
I know it is your Holy Spirit,
who shares the same nature with you, who
shares your honour,
O Word![1]

A close examination of Symeon's vision of divine light brings attention to the similarities between his vision and the events that took place in the upper room at Pentecost in Acts 2. In particular, I have always been fascinated by his seemingly paradoxical pairing of "intoxicating light" with "movements of fire." What does it mean to be intoxicated by light? Is that even really a thing? And how can we explain the swirling flame that Symeon says moves in him?

While some may say his statement sounds too charismatic or Pentecostal, most theologians and historians would agree that such statements are within the Christian tradition. For example, Symeon can speak of being intoxicated by light just as Peter in Acts 2:15 clarifies to the audience in Jerusalem that those who have received the Holy Spirit at Pentecost are not drunk as was supposed. Some may choose to parse the words "intoxication" and "drunk," asserting that intoxication is the more formal term while drunkenness speaks of external behavior. Whatever the case may be, Symeon clearly seems to believe it is possible to be intoxicated by the light that is the Holy Spirit, just as those surrounding the one hundred twenty in the upper room thought they were drunk at Pentecost.

But what does it mean to be intoxicated by light? In looking to provide a contemplative answer I am reminded of a statement from the Gospel of John that coincides with the third article of the Nicene Creed. According to John, "In him was life, and the life was the light of all people" (John 1:4). This life that is in Jesus is the life the Spirit gives, as the third article of the creed explains: "We believe in the Holy Spirit, the Lord, the giver of life." As Paul puts it, this is the same Holy Spirit "who raised Jesus from the dead" (Romans 8:11). Therefore, if the life that is in Jesus is through the Spirit (the giver of life) and yet that life is the light of men, it then follows that to be intoxicated with light (as Symeon suggests) is to be intoxicated in the newness of a life empowered by the Spirit as displayed at Pentecost!

Can you imagine the richness of this type of contemplative spirituality? In remembering and practicing Pentecost we are literally drinking from the fountain of a new and everlasting life of the Spirit, until that life becomes a light or fire (*phōs* in the Greek) that sheds light into our lives, intoxicating us. And just as the term *intoxication* suggests, we lose control in and to that light, which is the life of the Spirit that raised Jesus from the dead—and can raise you and me from any dead situation we might encounter. In celebrating Pentecost we are once again giving over control to the Spirit's life-giving power so we might become intoxicated with that newness of life, and consequently that life becomes our light in darkness.

As we have already discussed in the last chapter on rituals, the theme of celebrating life and renewal is connected to the use of the color green for Pentecost. In keeping with this theme, the prayers, Scriptures, and hymns in the Eastern Orthodox tradition embody a rich appreciation for the newness of life through the Spirit. In Eastern Orthodoxy, the celebration of Pentecost is usually done using the Pentecostarion, a liturgical book containing Scripture readings, hymns, and prayers for Pentecost.

Particularly for the Greek Orthodox Church of America, the Scriptures to be read during Saturday vespers—Numbers 11:16-17, 24-29; Joel 2:23-32; Ezekiel 36:24-28—are all preparatory Old Testament Scriptures. These passages call us to renew the importance we place on gathering and preparing in connection with the imagery of God's Spirit being poured out among those who gather, a foreshadowing of the coming of the Holy Spirit upon those gathered in Acts 2.

The next Scripture to be read during Pentecost in the Greek Orthodox tradition is John 20:19-23, which is to be read at Orthros (matins/mornings). This Scripture has been identified as John's version of Pentecost, which tells of how, when the disciples were gathered in a room with the doors locked "for fear of the Jews, Jesus came and stood among them and said, 'Peace be with you'" (John 20:19). Afterward Jesus shows his disciples his hands and his side, commissions them to go out, and breathes on them, saying, "Receive the Holy Spirit. If you forgive the sins of any, they are forgiven them; if you retain the sins of any, they are retained" (John 20:22-23).

This Scripture connects us with importance of forgiveness in relation to Pentecost and mirrors Peter's admonishment in the upper room: "Repent, and be baptized every one of you in the name of Jesus Christ so that your sins may be forgiven; and you will receive the gift of the Holy Spirit" (Acts 2:38).

The third set of Scripture readings is found within the actual Pentecost Sunday Divine Liturgy: Acts 2:1-11; John 7:37-52; 8:12. These particular Scriptures rehearse the Pentecost event found in Acts with the promise of the Holy Spirit found in the Gospel of John. In contrast to how Jesus presents the promise of the Holy Spirit in the Synoptic Gospels and in Acts, in the Gospel of John, Jesus' promise of the Holy Spirit on the last day of the Feast of Tabernacles is pronounced upon a crowd of people who then argue and become divided among themselves (John 7:43). One of the main points of reflection that should be taken from these Scriptures is that Jesus' promise of the Holy Spirit is made more broadly than to just his disciples and is similar to Joel's declaration:

Then afterward
I will pour out my spirit on all flesh;
your sons and your daughters shall prophesy,

your old men shall dream dreams,

and your young men shall see visions. (Joel 2:28)

Pentecost is most definitely the empowerment of the church toward the vision of the kingdom of God, yet Joel declares that the Spirit would be poured out "on all flesh." This raises a question: During Pentecost can we see God's Spirit at work in places and people outside of the church and its believers?

The last set of Scripture readings for Pentecost in the Greek Orthodox Church is found in the Divine Liturgy of the Monday of the Holy Spirit: Ephesians 5:8-19; Matthew 18:10-20.[2] These Scriptures deal with the question, now what? After Pentecost has come and after we have been filled with the Holy Spirit, what do we do now, and where do we go from here? Paul's admonishment to the church at Ephesus is that, now that we are in the light, we must "live as children of light—for the fruit of the light is found in all that is good and right and true" (Ephesians 5:8-9). Paul goes on to encourage the Ephesian believers to discover what the acceptable will of the Lord is (Ephesians 5:10), to have no fellowship with "unfruitful works of darkness" but rather to expose them and the people behind them (Ephesians 5:11-14), to utilize wisdom

(Ephesians 5:15), and to not be drunk with wine but filled with the Spirit, singing "psalms and hymns and spiritual songs among yourselves, singing and making melody to the Lord in your hearts" (Ephesians 5:19). This passage of Scripture is connected to the Matthean passage that calls us to consider the lost sheep (Matthew 18:10-14) as well as our sinning brother or sister (Matthew 18:15-20). These Scripture readings taken together provide believers with a blueprint for what to do and how to be after being filled with the power of the Spirit at Pentecost.

In keeping with Paul's admonishment to sing to each other psalms and hymns found in Ephesians 5, the Eastern Orthodox tradition features a number of hymns connected to the celebration of Pentecost. According particularly again to the Greek Orthodox Church of America, the first hymn connected to the celebration of Pentecost is the Kontakion, a poetic homily consisting of up to thirty stanzas. These stanzas, which are chanted, all follow the same structural pattern. Historians believe a soloist sang the main stanzas, while the choir responded with the refrain.[3] The Kontakion can be read, chanted, or sung as follows:

When the Most High came down and confounded tongues of men at Babel, He divided the nations. When

He dispensed the tongues of fire, He called all to unity,
and with one voice we glorify the Most Holy Spirit.[4]

This hymn not only recapitulates the Babel and Pentecost events by placing them in contrast (Babel division, Pentecost unity), but it also emphasizes our present reality: "With one voice we glorify the Most Holy Spirit." This hymn reminds us that no matter where we are in the world, and no matter what Christian tradition we belong to, at Pentecost all those who believe in the coming of the Holy Spirit sing and glorify the Most Holy Spirit, and God hears it as if it was coming from one voice.

The second hymn connected to the celebration of Pentecost in the Eastern Orthodox Church is the Apolytikion or, for the Orthodox Church of America, the Troparion. This is usually a dismissal hymn chanted at vespers and matins and within the Divine Liturgy. The Apolytikon summarizes the feast being celebrated, and in the case of Pentecost it reads as follows:

Blessed are You, O Christ our God, who made fishermen all-wise, by sending down upon them the Holy Spirit, and through them, drawing all the world into Your net. O Loving One, glory be to You.[5]

This second hymn reminds us that as we are sent forth into the world at the conclusion of our liturgies/services, our commission as fishers of humanity who have been empowered by the Spirit should be ever before us. Do you notice that in this hymn the net belongs to God and not the fisherman? This notion is probably taken from Old Testament Scriptures such as Psalm 66, which sees God as the fisherman and we the ones who have been brought into his net (Psalm 66:11). In the New Testament, however, Scriptures like Matthew 13:47—"Again, the kingdom of heaven is like a net that was thrown into the sea and caught fish of every kind"—remind us that the net we use to fish with (evangelize) is the kingdom of God.

Both chanted hymns, the Kontakion and the Apolytikon, are available to listen to at the Greek Orthodox Church of America's website at goarch.org/pentecost.

In the Eastern church, prayers said at Pentecost are known as "kneeling prayers," which follow the humble and penitent posture already discussed. These are usually three prayers varying in length that are prayed on either the Monday after Pentecost or on Pentecost Sunday after the actual Pentecost liturgy. In the Greek Orthodox tradition, for example, kneeling prayers are prayed during vespers the Monday after Pentecost immediately after the Divine Liturgy for Pentecost. In the Orthodox Church of America, kneeling prayers are also prayed during vespers and include an insightful array of Russian litanies.

Interestingly, none of the three prayers directly address the person of the Holy Spirit. Rather, the first prayer addresses God the Father as the source of the triune economy, while the second and the third prayers address the life and ministry of Jesus Christ his Son as empowered by the Holy Spirit. The three prayers offered here have been taken from Holy Trinity Church in Portland, Maine.[6] Only a few verses of their shortened versions are presented for practical use.

The first prayer. Not only does the first kneeling prayer address God the Father as the source of the triune economy, it also pleads with the Father that he might hear, forgive, and restore us:

> Hear us in your great mercy and love as we call upon you on this day of Pentecost, on which we remember how the Lord Jesus, after his ascension and sitting at your right hand, sent the Holy Spirit upon his holy disciples and apostles. They were filled with your inexhaustible grace and began speaking with other

tongues and prophesying, proclaiming your greatness. Hear us who pray to you, and remember us. Turn back the captivity of our souls and receive us as we return to you.

Interestingly, this section of the prayer addressed to the Father asks him to hear us as we call on him on the day of Pentecost, remembering how the Holy Spirit was sent by Jesus and how afterward the apostles were filled with "inexhaustible grace." This grace caused them to speak with other tongues and to prophesy, both actions proclaiming his greatness. The prayer then goes on to ask both for forgiveness and for the Father to receive us as we return to him.

This section of the first kneeling prayer in the Eastern Orthodox tradition reminds us of two things regarding Pentecost. First, speaking in tongues and prophesying in a way that proclaims the greatness of God the Father seems to be connected to God's "inexhaustible grace." Second, while this inexhaustible grace is obviously the source of our speaking and prophesying, it also seems inexhaustible inasmuch as we are not in sin and can be turned back and received by him.

At Pentecost, we acknowledge that our sins and our turning from God disconnect us from the inexhaustible grace that empowers us to communicate with other languages, cultures, and ethnicities as well as empowers us to forthtell what God is saying for his glory. These actions that come from the inexhaustible grace of God, a grace that never runs dry (2 Corinthians 9:8), are seemingly inaccessible to us when we are in sin and have turned our backs to God. Therefore, this section of the first kneeling prayer helps us understand that the power of Pentecost as experienced by the apostles through a grace-filled Spirit is limited to us only when our capacity for repentance is limited and restricted.

The second prayer. The second kneeling prayer, before addressing the life and ministry of Christ in the power of the Holy Spirit, recalls the Pentecost event in a manner more poignant than the first prayer:

Lord Jesus, you gave your peace to us, and you are always present to us, giving us the gift of the Holy Spirit. You sent down this grace in a manner most clear upon your holy disciples and apostles, and opened their lips with tongues of fire. Through them and others, the nations of the world have received the knowledge of God and have heard the message, each in their own language. We have been enlightened by the light of the Spirit, and we have been freed from delusion and darkness. Through the distribution of tongues of fire, we have been taught to worship one God in Trinity.

This particular section of the second prayer, just as the first, speaks of the Holy Spirit coming down as a grace upon the disciples and apostles, opening their lips with "tongues of fire." Most interesting, however, is the twofold consequence of this action. First, as we have already established, the nations received the knowledge of God in their own language. Second, and equally important, by the coming of the Holy Spirit in this manner we are enlightened by the light of the Holy Spirit and have been freed from both delusion and darkness.

Delusion and darkness! The word *darkness* in relation to the light of the Holy Spirit is straightforward in meaning. With confidence we can attribute darkness to our sinful state, our clouded judgment, and even our confused hearts, all of which need the illumination of the Spirit. But how can we interpret the word *delusion*? In what particular context does this kneeling prayer utilize it?

Delusion, according to most dictionaries, refers to something that is falsely believed or the act of tricking or deceiving someone. If this is the definition that's being used in the kneeling prayer, then the question we must ask is, what were we deluded about before the illumination of the Holy Spirit at Pentecost? Furthermore, what are we deluded about now that we are in need of the Spirit's illumination, just as in the day of Pentecost? Further examination of the prayer leads me to suggest that the primary way the word *delusion* is being used is in reference to all nations of the world receiving the knowledge of God, hearing it in their own language. We receive the knowledge of God through the illumination of the coming of the Spirit at Pentecost, and in fact we continue to need and receive this knowledge through illumination today.

This section of the second prayer also reminds us of the reversal of the nationalistic spirit present at the tower of Babel. At Pentecost we are awakened from the delusion that only our race, ethnicity, culture, political party, or language matters, is important, or is even truly Christian. This is one of the great errors of postmodernity, this division through delusion. In remembering Pentecost, however, we once again call on the Spirit to illuminate the dark areas of our lives and confront our delusion with godly wisdom and truth. As the next sentence in the prayer indicates, "May the Spirit of wisdom cover all my reasoning, and may my foolishness be overcome by the Spirit of understanding."

The third prayer. The third and final Pentecost kneeling prayer in the Eastern Orthodox tradition centers its focus around the salvific work of Christ, which destroys the bonds of death, tramples down evil spirits, and enlightens those who sit in darkness. It goes on to pray to the enlightener (Jesus) to help us with our temptations and prepare us for the end of all things and for the kingdom to come:

> Because you shared in our flesh, you are a Helper to us in our need and temptation, and you will also judge us with no partiality. There is no death for your servants, O Lord, when we go forth from the body and come unto you, but a change from things most sorrowful unto things most blessed and sweet and joyous. Forgive us, O Sinless One, of all the things which we have committed in your sight and grant us a good and peaceful end as you prepare for us your Kingdom.

While the first two kneeling prayers remind us of God's inexhaustible grace along with the Spirit's enlightenment of our delusion, this third prayer reminds us of the eschatological nature of Pentecost. Pentecost is not only empowerment for the present life and mission of the church but also speaks of the last days, as Peter exclaims in Acts 2:17:

In the last days it will be, God declares,

that I will pour out my Spirit upon all flesh,
  and your sons and your daughters shall
    prophesy,
and your young men shall see visions,
and your old men shall dream dreams.

Pentecost is empowerment and preparation for the world to come through the continual renewal or sanctification of our lives by the power of the Holy Spirit. It is the Spirit who sanctifies (1 Peter 1:2; 2 Thessalonians 2:13), who convicts the world of sin, and who guides us into all truth (John 16:8, 13). Therefore, Pentecost as the coming of the Spirit speaks of continual sanctification or, as many in the Orthodox Church know it, theosis. This process of deification speaks of a progression in perfection (1 Peter 1:16) that prepares us for the kingdom to come.[7]

As we discussed earlier, none of these kneeling prayers address the Holy Spirit directly. Yet there is a prayer Orthodox Christians pray at Pentecost that is devoted especially to the Spirit. It is called the Prayer of the Holy Spirit, and instead of being prayed only at Pentecost, it is commonly prayed in the weekly Orthodox liturgy. It opens the service of matins and many other services of the church, and it should be part of every person's prayer life. It reads as follows:

> O Heavenly King, the Comforter, the Spirit of Truth, Who art everywhere and fillest all things; Treasury of Blessings, and Giver of Life: come and abide in us, and cleanse us from every impurity, and save our souls, O Good One.

As a Pentecostal I have often been asked to preach or teach at events that emphasize the coming of the Holy Spirit. When I ask for the thematic details of the event so I might be better prepared to serve, I am often told by the coordinators that there is a need for an outpouring like the one on the day of Pentecost. Some clergy have even gone so far as to build and develop prayer and worship services specifically designed to relive and re-experience the Pentecost event.

The question I've always had was, if the Spirit already came at the day of Pentecost, aren't we supposed to move on in the world with him and in his power? Does it make sense to develop services designed to call down the power of the Spirit we already have? This prayer prayed by Orthodox Christians on a weekly basis reminds us of the fact that now, through the continual work and presence of the Spirit, every day, week, month, and year is its own Pentecost. No longer do we have to tarry, wait, or even long for the coming of the Holy Spirit as the faithful disciples did in the upper room, for now the Spirit is continually and faithfully with us.

A last insight regarding the Eastern Orthodox Pentecost liturgy is that, contrary to the Western Roman Catholic tradition, celebration of All Saints' Day falls on the first Sunday after Pentecost.[8] In so doing it places the Spirit at the center of the work and life of those who by his power have gone on to exhibit lives and ministries worthy of sainthood.

Roman Catholic

Similar to the Eastern Orthodox Church, the Roman Catholic celebration of Pentecost usually begins with a vigil the Saturday night before Pentecost. According to the Roman Missal, if the Pentecost vigil is in extended form (which also includes evening vespers), the service may begin by utilizing the hymn *Veni Creator Spiritus* ("Come Creator Spirit").[9] This hymn is believed to have been written by Rabanus Maurus, a ninth-century German monk, teacher, songwriter, and archbishop.

> Come, Holy Spirit, Creator blest, and in our souls
>   take up Thy rest;
> come with Thy grace and heavenly aid to fill the
>   hearts which Thou hast made.
> O comforter, to Thee we cry, O heavenly gift of
>   God Most High,
> O fount of life and fire of love, and sweet anointing
>   from above.
> Thou in Thy sevenfold gifts are known; Thou,
>   finger of God's hand we own;
> Thou, promise of the Father, Thou Who dost the
>   tongue with power imbue.
> Kindle our sense from above, and make our hearts
>   overflow with love;
> with patience firm and virtue high the weakness of
>   our flesh supply.
> Far from us drive the foe we dread, and grant us
>   Thy peace instead;

so shall we not, with Thee for guide, turn from the
      path of life aside.
Oh, may Thy grace on us bestow the Father and
      the Son to know;
and Thee, through endless times confessed, of
      both the eternal Spirit blest.
Now to the Father and the Son, Who rose from
      death, be glory given,
with Thou, O Holy Comforter,
henceforth by all in earth and heaven. Amen.

In singing the *Veni Creator Spiritus* I am reminded of a
few historic Christian themes that have captured the
Christian imagination for centuries. For example, the
theme of creation and rest as integrated in the first stanza
of the hymn reminds me of Saint Augustine's statement,
"You have made us for yourself O Lord, and our hearts are
restless until they rest in you."[10] Pentecost as recaptured
by the *Veni Creator Spiritus* causes us to go back and locate
the Spirit's presence as the blessed Creator hovering over
the waters in creation and yet calls for the same Spirit to
find its home in our hearts. Simultaneously, as Saint Augustine declares, we acknowledge that we who have been
created are restless until we find our home in our Creator.

A second important theme derived from the hymn in relation to Pentecost is the theme of the seven gifts of the Holy Spirit, as expressed by the statement, "Thou in Thy sevenfold gifts are known; Thou, finger of God's hand we own." This theme of the seven gifts of the Spirit, which we will explore in its prayer format later in this chapter, is prominent in Roman Catholic theology and spirituality and originates from Isaiah 11:1-2 (NKJV):

> There shall come forth a Rod from the stem of Jesse,
> And a Branch shall grow out of his roots.
> The Spirit of the LORD shall rest upon Him,
> The Spirit of wisdom and understanding,
> The Spirit of counsel and might,
> The Spirit of knowledge and of the fear of
>   the LORD.

Most interesting, however, is that in this passage we find the characteristics of the messianic figure to come (Jesus), each prefaced by the phrase "the Spirit of": wisdom, understanding, counsel, fortitude, knowledge, piety, and fear of God.[11] The Scripture, in capitalizing the word "Spirit," indicates a connection between the messianic figure and the Holy Spirit. Therefore, in singing the *Veni Creator*

Spiritus at Pentecost, Christians are reminded of the gifts of the Spirit needed to continue to proclaim and live out the gospel of Jesus Christ.

The last theme I would like to call our attention to from the *Veni Creator Spiritus* is its call to "kindle our sense from above." What sense could the hymn be referring to? Rudolf Otto, a twentieth-century theologian, is usually credited with coining the phrase *mysterium tremendum et fascinans* as a way of speaking of a holy and transcendent God who is a mystery humanity both trembles at and is fascinated by.[12] This is the sense I believe the hymn to be referring to. It is the sense of wonder, awe, fascination, and reverence for God—a sense that seems to be relaxed with every "God is my friend" book that comes along. No longer does it seem we approach God the Father with the reverence and awe with which the patriarchs and matriarchs of our faith approached God.

I can distinctly remember, when I was a child, there was a room on the first floor of the Pentecostal church I grew up in where people went to pray before the service started. Intrigued by its existence, I asked my grandmother why the room drew so many people in prayer when the sanctuary was upstairs. Her response was that people coming into the church would go into that room to pray and ask God for the forgiveness of their sins lest they enter the sanctuary having not repented of their sins and be called out.

You see, back then it was not uncommon for some of the older mothers of the church, women of prayer and fasting, to be caught up in a Spirit-filled moment during worship and have a word of knowledge, wisdom, or prophesy. Sometimes they would approach those with unrepented sins, disclosing them to the congregation and calling these believers to repentance. As children growing up in this environment, we learned to hold the presence of the Holy Spirit in reverence, and we stood in awe of a mystery we knew to be terrible and at the same time fascinating. In fact, after this conversation with my grandmother, I found myself in the prayer room asking God to forgive me of my sins.

When was the last time you rediscovered the terrible, tremendous, and fascinating nature of the mystery of God's presence? When was the last time you looked up to the stars or looked into a valley and lost your breath in awe of who God is? The *Veni Creator Spiritus* reminds us that at Pentecost, the coming of the Holy Spirit kindles our sense from above as we experience the duality of a mysterious God who is terrible, tremendous, and fascinating at the same time.

The *Veni Creator Spiritus,* which is sung at Pentecost vespers, should not be confused with the *Veni Sancte Spiritus,* which is usually sung during the mass on Pentecost Sunday. According to Robert Glendinning, author of *Early Christianity in Its Song and Verse*, composition of the *Veni Sancte Spiritus* has been attributed to three persons. In addition:

> [The *Veni Sancte Spiritus*] was composed to be sung as part of the liturgy of the Mass throughout the week preceding Pentecost, while the hymn of similar beginning, "O come, creator spirit, come" (*Veni Creator Spiritus*), by Hrabanus Maurus (Poem 25) was the hymn sung at Terce in monasteries and larger churches as part of the Divine Office of that week. The Pentecost sequence, "Holy Spirit, come, descend," was one of the most prized sequences of the Middle Ages and came to be known widely as the "Golden Sequence."[13]

After the *Veni Creator Spiritus* is sung and several rubrics have been completed (psalmody, priest's prayer and address to the people, and so on), there are several Scripture readings prescribed for Pentecost followed by prayers connected to the same. Similar to the 1979 Anglican Book of Common Prayer, the Gospel reading for the service of Pentecost, according to the Roman Missal, can be taken from either Acts 2 or the Gospel of John. In the Book of Common Prayer, the alternative Johannine reading is John 14:8-17.[14] The Roman Missal gives the choice of either John 7:37-39[15] or John 20:19-23.[16]

The first set of Scripture readings tackles the account of the tower of Babel (Genesis 11:1-9; Psalm 33:10-15). While the story of Babel itself can be read in the Genesis passage, the verses in Psalm 33 serve as an interpretation of that story, each one pointing to an aspect of the folly of those who built the tower:

> The LORD brings the counsel of the nations
>   to nothing;
> he frustrates the plans of the peoples.
> The counsel of the LORD stands forever,
> the thoughts of his heart to all generations.
> Happy is the nation whose God is the LORD,
> the people whom he has chosen as his heritage.

The LORD looks down from heaven;
he sees all humankind.
From where he sits enthroned he watches
all the inhabitants of the earth—
he who fashions the hearts of them all,
and observes all their deeds. (Psalm 33:10-15)

After this set of Scripture readings comes a prayer tied to the readings through the theme of unity and charity (two things obviously not found in the tower of Babel story). The prayer reads as follows:

Grant, we pray, almighty God,
that your Church may always remain that
     holy people,
formed as one by the unity of Father, Son and
     Holy Spirit,
which manifests to the world
the Sacrament of your holiness and unity
and leads it to the perfection of your charity.
Through Christ our Lord.
Amen.[17]

The second set of Pentecost Scripture readings deals mainly with God's descent on Mount Sinai in Exodus 19:3-8, a connection we have already explored. This

Scripture reading is accompanied by the Canticle (hymn) of Daniel 3:52-56, which is also known as the Song of Three Children and is taken from the book of Daniel in the Greek Apocrypha, which contained material not found in the original Hebrew. In the Apocrypha, after Daniel 3:23, the three "children" (Shadrach, Meshach, and Abednego) sing this song as they stand in Nebuchadnezzar's fiery furnace.[18] The song is not included in the canonical book of Daniel Protestants possess, but it is regarded as canonical by the Roman Catholic Church as well as the Eastern Orthodox Church. In the New Revised Standard Version Catholic Edition it reads:

> Blessed are you, O Lord, God of our ancestors,
> and to be praised and highly exalted forever;
> And blessed is your glorious, holy name,
> and to be highly praised and highly exalted forever.
> Blessed are you in the temple of your holy glory,
> and to be extolled and highly glorified forever.
> Blessed are you who look into the depths from
>   your throne on the cherubim,
> and to be praised and highly exalted forever.
> Blessed are you on the throne of your kingdom,

and to be extolled and highly exalted forever.
Blessed are you in the firmament of heaven,
and to be sung and glorified forever.
(Daniel 3:52-56 NRSVCE)

The Canticle of Daniel, although not in the accepted Protestant canon, still teaches us about the importance of being in God's presence in song. Just as Moses and the children of Israel were to be at Mount Sinai with God, who is "a consuming fire" (Hebrews 12:29) and whose very presence covered the mountain "like the smoke of a kiln" (Exodus 19:18), is how the three young boys were to be in the midst of the fiery furnace—and how we should be in times when we experience God in like manner. In such experiences we truly come to know God again as *mysterium, tremendum et fascinans.*

The second Scripture reading that accompanies the Mount Sinai narrative is Psalm 19:8-11. This particular Scripture deals with the statutes or commandments of the Lord and speaks to the keeping of the Ten Commandments Moses received:

The precepts of the LORD are right,
    rejoicing the heart;

the commandment of the LORD is clear,
>   enlightening the eyes;
the fear of the LORD is pure,
>   enduring forever;
the ordinances of the LORD are true
>   and righteous altogether.
More to be desired are they than gold,
>   even much fine gold;
sweeter also than honey,
>   and drippings of the honeycomb.

Moreover by them is your servant warned;
>   in keeping them there is great reward.
>   (Psalm 19:8-11)

After the Scripture readings comes a prayer that connects to them beautifully. This prayer ties the experience on Mount Sinai to the outpouring of the Spirit at Pentecost in a way that identifies the historic people of God as a multicultural community of the Spirit. It reads as follows:

O God, who in fire and lightning
gave the ancient Law to Moses on Mount Sinai
and on this day manifested the new covenant
in the fire of the Spirit, grant, we pray,

that we may always be aflame with that same Spirit
whom you wondrously poured out on your Apostles,
and that the new Israel,
gathered from every people,
may receive with rejoicing
the eternal commandment of your love.
Through Christ our Lord.
R. Amen.[19]

The third set of Scripture readings in the Roman Missal
for Pentecost Sunday has to do with God's Spirit and the
valley of dry bones in Ezekiel 37:1-14. Up to now we have not
looked at this particular narrative in relation to the Pentecost
event in Acts 2, but the similar demarcations are clear. In
Ezekiel 37 God brings the prophet in the Spirit out to a great
valley filled with dry bones, which he later discovers are the
"whole house of Israel" (Ezekiel 37:11). The prophet Ezekiel
is told by God to prophesy to these dry bones: "Thus says
the Lord GOD to these bones: I will cause breath to enter you,
and you shall live" (Ezekiel 37:5). The prophet does as he is
commanded, and "suddenly there was a noise, a rattling, and
the bones came together" (Ezekiel 37:7). Ezekiel goes on to
prophesy to the breath, "and they lived, and stood upon their
feet, an exceedingly great army" (Ezekiel 37:10 NKJV).

The similarities between the texts in Ezekiel 37 and Acts 2 are clear. Both events are empowered by the Spirit. Both include noises, and both include the Spirit's descent, which gives life. This notion of breath in relation to the season of Pentecost is originally found in Genesis 2:7, where God forms man out of the dust of the earth and breathes on him the breath of life, and man becomes a living soul.

According to Tertullian, the soul "has its origin in the breath of God,"[20] and according to Gregory of Nyssa, "God molds flesh like clay but makes the soul according to his image."[21] Thus the breath that brings man to life is a divine connection between humanity and the Creator, which no other creation is entitled to unlawfully or oppressively interfere with. Humankind receives through the breath of life a share of God's grace so that, according to Basil the Great, "Likeness might recognize Likeness."[22] This breath of life was given to humankind so that humankind might enjoy God, the creation, and each other. This grace is affected by the sin in the garden, and as a result there is a separation between humankind and God, humankind and creation, and humankind and each other. Thus humans are considered to have died and will continue to die, as the consequence shows.

This metaphor of "breath" in relation to Pentecost in Acts 2 and Ezekiel 37 is also what Jesus restores in the Gospel of John when he walks into the room where the disciples are hiding with the doors closed, pronounces peace, breathes on them, and declares, "Receive the Holy Spirit" (John 20:22). This is Pentecost in the Gospel of John. In breathing upon his disciples Jesus returns to them the breath given to humanity at creation so they can once again become alive not only in body but in soul as well (Ephesians 2:1-10).

Pentecost through Acts 2 and Ezekiel 37 reminds us that the breath of life, given to all human beings at birth, is sacred. Against the onslaught of violence—whether it be by way of police brutality, homicide, or substance abuse—these Pentecost Scriptures remind us of the importance of the wind that blew in the upper room just as the wind that blew in the nostrils of the first human being. Breath is sacred, and thus we are admonished, "Let everything that has breath praise the LORD" (Psalm 150:6 NKJV).

Psalm 107:2-9, the accompanying Scripture for the narrative in Ezekiel 37, helps to paint a broader picture for the believer. The psalm begins by identifying the redeemed as ones who have been

> gathered in from the lands,
>
> from the east and from the west,
>
> from the north and from the south. (Psalm 107:3)

This is similar to the breath that comes from the "four winds" in Ezekiel 37:9. The people described in Psalm 107 have wandered in the wilderness, found no city to dwell in, been hungry and thirsty, fainted in their souls, cried out to God, and been delivered of their distress (Psalm 107:4-9). It is then those in Psalm 107 whom Ezekiel in chapter 37 discovers as the whole house of Israel. And it is those whom the Spirit must visit once more in Acts 2.

These Scripture readings have three different prayer options in the Roman Missal. The first has to do with restoring what has fallen and preserving what has been restored:

> Lord, God of power,
>
> who restore what has fallen
>
> and preserve what you have restored,
>
> increase, we pray, the peoples
>
> to be renewed by the sanctification of your name,
>
> that all who are washed clean by holy Baptism
>
> may always be directed by your prompting.
>
> Through Christ our Lord.
>
> R. Amen.[23]

The second prayer has to do with rebirth and the pouring out of the Holy Spirit in order that we might attain the glory of the resurrection:

O God, who have brought us to rebirth by the
        word of life,
pour out upon us your Holy Spirit,
that, walking in oneness of faith,
we may attain in our flesh
the incorruptible glory of the resurrection.
Through Christ our Lord.
R. Amen.[24]

Similar to the second prayer, the final prayer following the third set of Scripture readings has to do mainly with rejoicing in the hope of the resurrection:

May your people exult for ever, O God,
in renewed youthfulness of spirit,
so that, rejoicing now in the restored glory of
        our adoption,
we may look forward in confident hope
to the rejoicing of the day of resurrection.
Through Christ our Lord.
R. Amen.[25]

The fourth and last set of Scripture readings found in the Roman Missal for the celebration of Pentecost has to do mainly with the great day of the Lord (Joel 3:1-5; Acts 2:20), which is a continuation of the Spirit being poured out on all flesh (Joel 2:28). This third chapter of Joel has similarities to Pentecost in Acts 2, in that dealing with "enemy" nations after the Spirit is poured out (Joel 3:1-5) connects to Peter's statement in Acts 2:34-35:

> The Lord said to my Lord,
> "Sit at my right hand,
> Until I make your enemies your footstool."

The enemies with whom God enters into judgment in Joel 3 are those who have scattered Israel among the nations and divided up God's land (Joel 3:2), have given children as payment for pleasures (Joel 3:3-4), and have taken God's silver and gold, carrying them away into their own temples (Joel 3:4-5). The accompanying Scripture reading to Joel 3:1-5 is a set of verses from Psalm 104: verses 1-2, 24, 35, 27-28, 29-30. These verses mainly recount the glory and majesty of God in relation to creation itself.

The last prayer connected to the concluding set of Scripture readings asks of God that he fulfill his promise concerning the outpouring of his Spirit so we might be effective witnesses in the world:

> Fulfill for us your gracious promise,
> O Lord, we pray, so that by his coming
> the Holy Spirit may make us witnesses before
>   the world
> to the Gospel of our Lord Jesus Christ.
> Who lives and reigns for ever and ever.
> R. Amen.[26]

Finally, as we briefly discussed earlier, one of the hymns sung frequently at the Roman Catholic celebration of Pentecost is the Prayer for the Seven Gifts of the Holy Spirit. The basis for this hymn, according to Glendinning, is found in Isaiah 11:2, a passage that has been taken to presage the future Messiah and his work of redemption. The "gifts" bestowed on Christian believers at Pentecost and believed to make them more susceptible to the action of divine grace are wisdom, understanding, counsel, fortitude, knowledge, piety (godliness), and fear of the Lord.[27] The hymn reads as follows:

> O Lord Jesus Christ, Who, before ascending into
>   heaven, didst promise to send the Holy Ghost

to finish Thy work in the souls of Thy
Apostles and Disciples, deign to grant the
same Holy Spirit to me, that He may perfect
in my soul the work of Thy grace and Thy love.

Grant me the Spirit of Wisdom that I may despise
the perishable things of this world and aspire
only after the things that are eternal,

the Spirit of Understanding to enlighten my mind
with the light of Thy divine truth,

the Spirit of Counsel that I may ever choose the
surest way of pleasing God and gaining
Heaven,

the Spirit of Fortitude that I may bear my cross with
Thee, and that I may overcome with courage
all the obstacles that oppose my salvation,

the Spirit of Knowledge that I may know God and
know myself and grow perfect in the science
of the Saints,

the Spirit of Piety that I may find the service of
God sweet and amiable,

the Spirit of Fear that I may be filled with a loving
reverence towards God, and may dread in
any way to displease Him.

Mark me, dear Lord, with the sign of Thy true
disciples and animate me in all things with
Thy Spirit. Amen.[28]

SYRIAN ORTHODOX

For Malankara Orthodox Syrian Christians, the service of
Pentecost consists of three parts, the first part addressed
to the Father, the second to the Son, and the third to the
Holy Spirit. At the conclusion of the service, during the
celebration of the Holy Eucharist, a bowl with pure water
and a bunch of green leaves used to sprinkle the water are
placed on the first step (Derga) of the altar at each of the
three services.[29] All three services include Scripture
readings and various prayers, including a prayer of abso-
lution and an incense prayer or *etro*, as well as a number
of hymns.[30] Most interesting and worthy of notice in the
Malankara Syrian Orthodox Pentecost liturgy of Saint
Gregorios Indian Orthodox Church in Mississauga,
Canada, are what they call *kolos/qolos* or hymns addressed
to the person of the Holy Spirit found in all three services
and the *eniyonos*, which are responses by the congregation
to the Scripture read by the clergy,[31] or mediative songs,[32]
found in the first service. These sometimes unconsidered

prayers and responses are noteworthy for their rich, vibrant, and creative pneumatological presence. The following are the three *kolos*/hymns each in their order. The wording has been formatted for better presentation and I provide a brief inspirational and devotional commentary at the end of each one:

Syrian Orthodox Kolo No. 1

Holy Spirit descended this day from the heights
  of heaven
Mingled with men to make them all children of
  one Holy God
Blessed God kept His promise
To send comforter Spirit
And gave tongues to preach nations
Blessed is Lord who revealed—Mystery of Trinity.

Like a fiery tongue Holy Ghost—Appeared to
  disciples
They proclaimed to nations of world—Holy and
  three sacred names
In one Thy body and blood
Other disciples got strengthened
With Holy spirit two feasts

Lord who gifted is blessed—Praise to Thee for
     gifts indeed.

When holy apostles received—Comforter from
     Most High God
They began speaking in new tongues—And
     obtained mystical strength
Went out to proclaim Gospel
Comforting the creations
And made all their disciples
By baptizing them in name—of Father, Son,
     Holy Ghost.

God who talked to Moses on the—Burning bush
     at Mount Sinai
To release Israelites from—Their slavery in Egypt
Fortress for Kings of whole world
May safeguard His Holy Church
Let us praise Holy, majestic
Father, Son and Holy Ghost—Three in one
     the Trinity.[33]

This first Pentecost hymn covers many of the aspects
we have already discussed in other traditions, including
diverse languages (tongues) as portrayed in Acts 2 for the

purpose of spreading the gospel to all nations. The hymn also connects the Mount Sinai narrative to the Pentecost narrative in Acts 2, along with the nature of the Trinity. One of the more interesting phrases in this particular hymn is "an obtained mystical strength" in reference to speaking in new tongues. One can only surmise that the hymn is making reference to the gifts of the Spirit seen operating in the book of Acts after the coming of the Holy Spirit as acts directed toward evangelization of the gospel. Yet how often do we consider the mystical aspects of a spirituality birthed at Pentecost? And in what ways can we as Christians who commemorate and practice Pentecost be considered mystical? What role or impact does Pentecost play in our contemplative spirituality, which leads us to broader reflections about God and the human soul in worship? This hymn/prayer reminds us of that very supernatural power of the Holy Spirit that still operates today, both in our own personal lives and in the world through the church.

Syrian Orthodox Kolo No. 2

O—Lord and God—On this holy day of
Pentecosti—Seven weeks' festival,
Like flaming fire—Fluttered down Holy spirit

In upper room—On the Disciples.
And perfected—them in the one true faith and
Filled them with love—Hope and all virtues.
Made them whole and—They went to preach
     the virtues
To the lost ones—And redeemed them all.

O—Lord and God—On Thy day of ascension
Thou hast promised—Thy apostles that
Upon reaching—Father, I will send to you
Holy spirit—Who will make you all
Firm in mind and—teach you the Holy mystery
Which will strengthen—To fight evil one.
Hallclujah—You will teach the true faith to
Those who were fallen from one—true faith.

O—Lord and God—On this holy day of
Pentecosti—We beseeching You
To —pour on us—Your comforter Holy Spirit
And strengthen us—to fight evil one
Halleluiah—Make us worthy to worship
And adore the—Holy Trinity.

O—Apostles—Architects of one true faith
Who has built the—One and Holy Church,

Rejoice today—In wine of the life giving
Holy Spirit—to become—light for
Those who live in—darkness and teach them about
Greatest and Mystical Trinity
One—in three and—three in one Father, Son and
The Holy Ghost—Proclaim and adore.[34]

This second hymn brings together a complex body of Pentecost themes, including Pentecost as a seven-week festival, Christ's ascension, and filling up on the Holy Spirit like wine. If the first hymn/prayer reminds of the supernatural and mystical power of the Holy Spirit poured out on Pentecost, this second hymn calls our attention to the notion of true faith.

When viewed through the lens of Peter's Pentecost sermon, this hymn reminds us of the importance of orthodox teaching and faith, and it compels us in the power of the Spirit to teach the faith even to those who have fallen from it. In so doing, according to this hymn, we follow the lead of the holy apostles, who in the power of the Spirit that fell on Pentecost built the church through the same one true faith. Sadly, while the power of the Spirit that came upon the apostles on the day of Pentecost empowered them to teach the faith to those who had fallen away in the nations, today it seems the Pentecost power we need is for teaching the faith to those who have fallen away in the church.

Syrian Orthodox Kolo No. 3

On this sacred holy day—Comforter Holy Spirit
Descended like fiery tongues—Appeared to
    Disciples
They were strengthened with courage
They went preached to creation
Mystery of Trinity—Father, Son and Holy Ghost.

When disciples came forth to—Receive promised
    gift from God
Holy Spirit came to them—From heaven like fiery
    tongues
Enlightened their minds and hearts
Gave them wisdom to proclaim
Gospel through out the whole world—Fighting
    wicked's temptation.

Comforter Holy Spirit—Came to Holy Disciples
Told in different tongues of world—The most
    sacred mystery
Powered them to redeem sins

And for healing the sickness
In—name of the Trinity—Father, Son and
      Holy Ghost.

On—this Holy Sacred day—Mystery was revealed to
Holy disciples in the—Upper room by Holy Ghost
Descended like fiery tongues
Gave them power, help, wisdom
Perfected them with—Blessings from the most
      high God.[35]

This third and final Syrian Orthodox Pentecost hymn/ prayer combines themes from both the first and the second hymn (fiery tongues, proclamation of the gospel, and so on) and adds the themes of wisdom, enlightenment, and healing. These themes, although not readily displayed in Acts 2, are nevertheless works of the Spirit poured out at Pentecost.

Anglican

The Anglican tradition has a long, rich, and varied history of liturgical prayers for celebrating Pentecost. The Church of England, which baptizes as well as confirms believers at Pentecost, uses this most glorious prayer from the 1928 Book of Common Prayer for the sacrament of confirmation on Pentecost: "Defend, O Lord, these your servants with your heavenly grace, that they may continue yours forever, and daily increase in your Holy Spirit more and more, until they come to your everlasting kingdom. Amen."[36]

This prayer, simplistic as it may seem, is replete with wonderful biblical meaning. In particular, the notion of defense within the prayer reminds me of the connection that Gregory of Nyssa makes between the mystery of initiation (baptism, confirmation, and Eucharist) and God's protection for the Israelites as they crossed the Red Sea: "No one who hears this should be ignorant of the mystery of the water. He who has gone down into it with the army of the enemy emerges alone, leaving the enemy's army drowning in the water."[37]

What a thought! At Pentecost we are once again reminded that in the sacraments of initiation we have been defended from the foes and enemies of our life. These foes are not necessarily people, for as we are reminded our "struggle is not against flesh and blood" (Ephesians 6:12 NIV). Our foes are anything that opposes itself to our successfully lived Christian spirituality. In baptism, they (bills, stresses, anxieties, etc.) go down with us and are overtaken by the rushing of the many waters. Then, in confirmation we are reminded of that same fact and given the opportunity to dry off from our own immersion into new life. Lastly, at the Eucharist we are brought into the house of God and seated at a table that has been prepared for us in the presence of our enemies.

These prayers immerse Anglican believers (as well as others who draw from Anglican spiritualty) into the imaginative depth and breadth of the riches of the historic Christian tradition.

Anglicanism is also rich in hymns that celebrate almost every Christian aspect of life under the sun. One beloved Pentecost hymn in the Anglican tradition is "Hail This Joyful Day's Return," which stands out among the rest as a masterpiece of liturgical composition and for its interconnection with contemporary spirituality. The words are attributed to Hilary of Poitiers, and the traditional melody dates from the sixteenth century:

> Hail this joyful day's return,
> hail the Pentecostal morn,
> morn when our ascended Head
> on his Church his Spirit shed!

Like to cloven tongues of flame
on the twelve the Spirit came;
tongues, that earth may hear the call;
fire, that love may burn in all. . . .

Lord, to Thee Thy people bend,
unto us Thy Spirit send;
blessings of this sacred day
grant us, dearest Lord, we pray.

Thou who didst our [forebears] guide,
with their children still abide;
grant us pardon, grant us peace,
till our earthly wanderings cease.[38]

This hymn begins its first stanza with a creation-like scene where one's imagination could be taken to a dark morning awaiting the sunrise. The sheer celebratory energy presented here should develop excitement in every Christian believer for what is to come on the day of Pentecost: "Hail this joyful day's return, hail the Pentecostal morn." Pentecost should remind us of our Christian longing for the presence of the Spirit. It speaks of our tenacity through the struggles of the dark nights full of anxiety, confusion, and pain. Yet, as the psalmist reminds us, "Weeping may linger for the night / but joy comes with the morning" (Psalm 30:5).

The first stanza of this Pentecost hymn also reveals to us a great revelation regarding the sending of the Spirit: "Morn when our ascended Head on his Church his Spirit shed!" When I read this verse, I'm reminded that Pentecost occurs because Jesus our Lord asks his Father to pour down the Holy Spirit after his ascension (see John 14:16-30). The Holy Spirit is poured out on the church of the ascended, victorious Jesus at Pentecost.

If there was ever a verse in an Anglican hymn that captured the essence, nature, and purpose for the tongues spoken at Pentecost it would be the second stanza of this hymn: "Like to cloven tongues of flame on the twelve the Spirit came—tongues, that earth may hear the call; fire, that love may burn in all."

Amazing! The thought of tongues of fire coming to the earth at Pentecost so that the Earth may hear their call can and must be interpreted holistically to include not only every nation, tribe, and people group, but also include creation itself, which is awaiting the revealing of the sons and daughters of God with its own groaning and moaning (see Romans 8:19-22). At Pentecost, the languages that were spoken brought unity in horizontal relationships with others as well as a vertical relationship with God. This particular stanza helps to remind us that there is yet another level of unity: unity with the earth itself. Here, Pentecost becomes part of the broader ecological conversation for Christians. Just as there is divine and anthropological communication at Pentecost, there is also ecological communication brought about by the same event as a holistic embodiment of the gospel. In short, at Pentecost God speaks to us, we speak to each other, and the earth—hearing the call of the sons and daughters of God—speaks to us in return, yearning for our great reveal.

The last two stanzas in this wonderful hymn speak to us of Pentecost as a time of granted prayer and also as a reminder of how the Spirit is our peace and guide on our earthly pilgrimage. This reminder comes not only with a focus on the present but also with a plea that we be granted pardon, brought to peace, and be guided just as our forebears were guided, pardoned, and brought to peace. As Peter remembered, it was the prophet Joel who spoke of the Spirit being poured out on the last days.

Pentecost is the day when we ought to not only reflect on the goodness of God's spirit in the present but also on his abiding power and pardon present in our Christian past. There, we are reminded of the throngs of believers (many persecuted and martyred) who make up the great cloud of witnesses who have been pardoned, protected, guided, and provided peace from their labor. Our thoughts at Pentecost should always be that if God through his Spirit kept our antecedents, then surely he will keep us.

This Pentecost, as you reflect on this Anglican hymn, may its literary marvel remind you that every dark night has a morning burning with light and radiance. May you also be reminded of your role as a believer empowered by the Holy Spirit to an earth in need of your witness. And may you be reminded that just as God has kept those in your past, he by his Spirit, descended on those gathered at Pentecost, will surely and without a doubt keep you.

Pentecostal

As a Pentecostal Christian I would be remiss if I did not, one, speak out of my own context regarding Pentecost and, two, explore how Pentecostals celebrate Pentecost and exhibit Pentecost-ish spirituality. I was raised in one of the largest Pentecostal denominations in the world.

But to say I was disconnected from the liturgical season of Pentecost would be an understatement. In fact, had someone told me of the liturgical season of Pentecost back then, my response would have been that we practiced and experienced Pentecost every week at church.

By this I mean I grew up personally experiencing ecstatic manifestations of the Spirit such as tongues, miracles, gifts of prophecy, gifts of interpretation, and healings every Sunday. In fact, I remember vividly how one Sunday our pastor stood in front of a large window in the sanctuary, allowing the sun to hit his back and causing a shadow to form on the ground. In this position he exclaimed, "Let all who want to be healed come in contact with my shadow!" This act mirrors the narrative found in Acts 5 where people are healed by Peter's shadow. At other times we saw oil dripping from the walls and heard testimonies of people receiving healings from things like dental pain and cancer.

The miracles, signs, and wonders that mirrored the miracles, signs, and wonders found in the book of Acts were every-week occurrences at the church where I grew up, but we gave no consideration to the liturgical celebration of Pentecost. To be clear, Pentecostalism as a religious movement birthed in the twentieth century has not historically followed the liturgical Christian calendar. Segments of Pentecostalism today are recovering the treasures of the church's historic liturgy, but by and large Pentecostalism still does not engage in liturgical practices. Yet there are other more experiential practices within Pentecostal spirituality that speak to the Pentecost event in Acts 2. In addition to the many songs sung in the Pentecostal tradition that refer to the events of Acts 2, there are two types of spirituality seen in almost all Pentecostal churches that stem directly from the New Testament account of Pentecost.

The first of these experiences directly correlated to Acts 2 is the baptism in the Holy Spirit. The notion of being baptized in the Holy Spirit, at least for the majority of classical Pentecostals whose heritage is the Azusa Street Revival of the 1900s, is inherited from the Wesleyan "second work" theology. According to James Smith, this theology "emphasized an experience of grace and sanctification subsequent to and distinct from salvation."[39] Usually in classical Pentecostal circles the baptism in the Holy Spirit is evidenced by speaking in tongues or, as it is identified in theological circles, glossolalia.

The notion of tongues as evidence of the baptism in the Holy Spirit has not been universally accepted. For years there has been a debate within Pentecostalism about what should be the identifying marker of being baptized in the Holy Spirit as a second work of grace. Some have suggested the presence of the fruit of the Spirit, while others have believed that love is the evidence. Whatever the case may be, being baptized in the Holy Spirit is a biblical (Matthew 3:11; John 1:33; Acts 1:4-5) and experiential part of Pentecostal spirituality that all Pentecostals are admonished and encouraged to pursue.

My own baptism in the Holy Spirit took place when I was nineteen and attending a youth revival meeting in New York. I had just come back to the church after re-dedicating my life to Christ, and my father told me about this youth revival and encouraged me to go. Two days earlier we had visited with my grandparents in New Jersey, and the first night there I had spent some time in prayer and reflection before going to bed. After praying for about an hour, I sensed an urge to open the Bible and read the first thing that came up. Now, I had heard of this type of occurrence from other people who claimed to have received a word from the Lord when they opened their

Bible, but that had never been my experience. But that night after prayer I just opened the Bible, stuck my finger on a page, and read the first thing I saw. The Scripture my finger was pointing to was Acts 1:5 (NKJV): "For John truly baptized with water, but you shall be baptized with the Holy Spirit not many days from now."

At this point I was confused and intrigued all at the same time. What could this mean? I had seen others baptized in the Spirit but had never experienced it myself. Could God be telling me I was going to be baptized in the Spirit? After resting that night and the following night, the day finally arrived for the youth revival. When I showed up I was skeptical, and I could see that some who knew of my past were uncomfortable to see me there. Still, I put on the best face I could, worshiped, heard the sermon, and even reacted positively to the altar call afterward. Then, out of nowhere, the preacher looked into the crowd and said, "There are people here who God promised would be baptized in the Holy Ghost, and you can't leave here tonight without your promise."

Immediately it was as if I became paralyzed, with a warm feeling shooting up and down all through my body. The preacher then asked those who had been baptized in the Holy Spirit to form a line on each side, making a path in the middle for those who wanted the baptism in the Holy Spirit to walk through while they prayed and asked God on their behalf. I don't remember how, but even before the preacher finished speaking, I was already standing in line. It was as though my body understood something I myself didn't. When it was my turn, I didn't hesitate.

Have you ever had the feeling that something greater than you had overtaken you by invitation? An experience that even if you were to live a thousand lifetimes you would never forget? That was my experience with the baptism in the Holy Spirit that night. As I walked into the path the others had made, with young people on all sides praying for me, I said, "Holy Spirit, I need you."

And then it happened. It was as if a tornado and a calm, loving breeze perfectly collided in my body and soul, imprinting me with a code that would never go away. I had only felt that on two other occasions, and one of them was my water baptism. My mouth started speaking things my ears couldn't understand, but somehow it felt as though my soul understood, and it was the one having the conversation.

Afterward I was different. Truth be told, I'm still different. I still feel that warm sensation running through my body at worship. I still feel the conviction of the Spirit's presence when I'm being less than a good Christian. I still thank God every day for the power and presence of the Holy Spirit.

My experience is not the norm nor is it a universal indicator of the presence of the Holy Spirit. For years I have been privileged to hear other people's stories in relation to their experience of baptism in the Holy Spirit. Some experience tears and warmth of heart. Others experience deep conviction or peace. However it plays out, the baptism in the Holy Spirit within the Pentecostal tradition is a cherished experience that, when undergone, one never forgets.

In addition to the baptism in the Holy Spirit, the "tarrying service" is another Pentecostal tradition with parallels to the events at Pentecost in Acts 2. In this service believers linger or delay at the altar until the Spirit shows up. This notion of delay until one is filled with the Spirit stems directly from Jesus' command to his disciples to wait or tarry in Luke 24:49, as well as in the book of Acts: "While staying with them, he ordered them not to leave Jerusalem, but to wait there for the promise of the Father. 'This,' he said, 'is what you have heard from me'" (Acts 1:4).

Teresa L. Reed describes the development of the tarrying service ritual in the African American Pentecostal church as follows:

Candidates who were ready to be filled with the Holy Ghost (the next step after conversion and sanctification) would gather at the Saturday night prayer meeting designated specifically for this purpose. Typically, the tarrying service would begin when a song leader initiated a repetitive, call-and-response, congregational song, usually to the accompaniment of hand-claps, foot-stomps, tambourines, drums, and keyboard instruments. To the sound of this music, the "seekers" would be encircled and encouraged by helpers who assisted with prayer and praise until the achievement of infilling became evident. Often, the text of the opening song would give way to the rhythmic, continual repetition of the phrase "Thank you Jesus." After continuous repetition of the phrase, the evidence of the candidate's infilling (or possession) by the Holy Ghost was in whether or not he or she spoke in tongues.[40]

The tarrying service continues to be a rite in many Pentecostal congregations birthed out of the Pentecost event in Acts 2. From Melvin Butler:

> Most Pentecostals acknowledge that tarrying, in the sense of a prolonged period of waiting, is not at all necessary once an individual's heart is properly geared toward God. However, tarry services continue to constitute a major component of Pentecostal services, not only in Jamaica, but also throughout the African Diaspora.[41]

This general Pentecostal spiritual practice, although it also occurs outside the season of Pentecost, stems directly from it. Tarrying, although done with ecstatic zeal and passion in the Pentecostal tradition, is no less a reality and a divine notion practiced by those at Pentecost. Today it continues to speak to believers of the value of waiting on God for the promises of God even through times of difficulty. While for Pentecostals the promise of the Holy Spirit comes through the presence of manifested spiritual gifts, for others the promise comes in the assurance that he will never leave us nor forsake us (Hebrews 13:5) and that in his stead he has sent us the Comforter, Advocate, and Helper (John 14:16; 16:7).

Besides the baptism in the Holy Spirit and tarrying as a spiritual practice connected to Pentecost, there are other more subtle practices within Pentecostalism that correspond to the liturgical celebration in one way or another. For example, in my own personal experience with some African American Pentecostal churches, I have discovered that they wear white on Pentecost—not to commemorate baptism per se but to express purity and racial dignity. These themes are also connected to the Pentecost event even if they are expressed culturally. Another subtle Pentecostal practice connected to the Pentecost event is the fiery, passionate, and bold preaching of the gospel. This practice mirrors Peter's bold and raised proclamation after the descent of the Holy Spirit in Acts 2:14.

Conclusion

I magine having been invited to chill out in a room with people you know. You've waited in this room for about fifty days on and off, coming back and forth from work and home to be assembled with everyone, all on the promise that one day . . . some type of power would come.

Suddenly and unexpectedly, you hear a sound that can only compare with what it would sound like if a large wind turbine were to burst into the room where you were gathered. At this point you and those sitting around you are struggling to maintain your sitting posture. As if that weren't enough, afterward you start to see visions of flames sitting on everyone's heads and to hear those around you speaking in other tongues.

What would your response be? The narration seems so odd to Christian believers in the twenty-first century, and yet how many of us, if it happened today, could explain what it meant? Pentecost remains a powerful mark in the church's calendar precisely because it continues to be beyond human control. There is nothing we can successfully rationalize or theologize about Pentecost that would cause all Christian parties to nod with complete approval, yet there is nothing we can do or say against it that discredits its success in evangelizing the nations.

In English, the word "Pente-Cost" can be thought of as the event in the Christian calendar that costs us fifty days of unburdening ourselves from the divisions and difficulties brought about by differences in race, culture, and religion. It is then and only then that we can expect the coming of the All Holy Spirit who empowers our hearts and lives so we might be better witnesses.

In concluding this work, my prayer is that humanity would embrace the cultural, religious, and ethnic diversity the Spirit empowers. When Jesus tells his disciples, "You will be my witnesses in Jerusalem, in all Judea and Samaria, and to the ends of the earth" (Acts 1:8), it is on the heels of the disciples receiving power when the Holy Spirit came upon them. And even then this power given to us by the Spirit is for being "witnesses," which in Greek is the word *martys,* from which we get our English word "martyr." In other words, to be a witness empowered by the Holy Spirit at Pentecost is to be an empowered martyr.

A martyr is one who understands that death is the greatest witness to belief. Today Christian martyrdom is rare in most of the Western Hemisphere. The question I'm frequently asked by people who hear me tackle this subject is, What do we die for? How do we die? I answer that the question is not what we die for or even how. That has been answered. The question we must ask ourselves as we tackle our spirituality in conjunction with the global city is, What do we die *to* so the power of Pentecost might flow through us?

May this Pentecost season bring you power, peace, and prosperity of soul. And may you remember to live in that power as you go about living intoxicated in the light that is the newness of life in the Spirit. Amen.

Notes

THE POWER OF PENTECOST

[1]W.E. Vine, *Vine's Expository Dictionary of Old and New Testament Words* (Nashville, TN: Thomas Nelson Publishers, 1997), 868-69.

[2]"Dunamis," Bible Study Tools, accessed February 10, 2022, www.bible studytools.com/lexicons/greek/nas/dunamis.html.

[3]Brigid C. Harrison, *Power and Society: An Introduction to the Social Sciences* (Boston: Cengage Learning, 2017), chap. 1, Kindle.

[4]I do believe there are some positive elements of the deconstruction movement, including the questioning of long-held social, political, and racial assumptions.

[5]Laurence Hull Stookey, *Calendar: Christ's Time for the Church* (Nashville, TN: Abingdon, 1996), 73.

[6]Arthur Wallis, "Revival and Recovery," in Frank Bartleman, *Azusa Street* (New Kensington, PA: Whitaker House Publishers, 1982), 158.

[7]Peter G. Cobb, "The History of the Christian Year," in *The Study of Liturgy*, ed. Cheslyn Jones et al., rev. ed. (New York: Oxford University Press, 1992), 463.

[8]Jean Daniélou, *The Bible and the Liturgy* (Notre Dame, IN: University of Notre Dame Press, 1961), 319.

[9]Daniélou, *Bible and Liturgy*, 320.

[10]Thomas S. Bremer, "Pilgrim or Tourist: How Do We Know the Difference?," Thomas S. Bremer (website), November 8, 2017, www.tsbremer .com/pilgrim-or-tourist.

1. Pentecost

[1]David Brickner and Rich Robinson, *Christ in the Feast of Pentecost* (Chicago: Moody Publishers, 2008), 22-23.

[2]Paul F. Bradshaw and Maxwell E. Johnson, *The Origins of Feasts, Fasts and Seasons in Early Christianity* (Collegeville, MN: Liturgical Press, 2011), 69.

[3]Bradshaw and Johnson, *The Origins of Feasts,* 70.

[4]Abraham Joshua Heschel, *The Sabbath* (New York: Farrar, Straus and Giroux), prologue, Kindle.

[5]Brickner and Robinson, *Christ in the Feast of Pentecost,* 29.

[6]Brickner and Robinson, *Christ in the Feast of Pentecost,* 28.

[7]Elisabeth Elliot, *Shadow of the Almighty: The Life and Testament of Jim Elliot* (New York: HarperSanFrancisco Publishers, 1989), 85.

[8]Clement of Alexandria, *Stromates,* VI, XI.

[9]Origen, *Homilies on Genesis II,* 5.

[10]Brickner and Robinson, *Christ in the Feast of Pentecost,* 35.

[11]Cyril of Alexandria, *De Adoratione in spiritu et veritate* (P.G. LXVIII, 1093).

[12]Jean Daniélou, *The Bible and the Liturgy* (Notre Dame, IN: University of Notre Dame Press, 1961), 323.

[13]Brickner and Robinson, *Christ in the Feast of Pentecost,* 27.

[14]"Old Testament Laws: Harvest Seasons of Ancient Israel," Article Archive, Grace Communion International, accessed August 8, 2022, archive.gci.org/articles/harvest-seasons-of-ancient-israel.

[15]Sejin Park, *Pentecost and Sinai: The Festival of Weeks as a Celebration of the Sinai Event* (New York: T&T Clark, 2008), 9.

2. Learning to Speak in Other Tongues

[1]Morton Kelsey, *Tongue Speaking: The History and Meaning of Charismatic Experience* (New York: Crossroad, 1981), 33.

[2]Irenaeus, *Against Heresies III,* 12.15.

[3]For an in-depth examination see Kelsey, *Tongue Speaking.*

[4]Laurence Hull Stookey, *Calendar: Christ's Time for the Church* (Nashville, TN: Abingdon, 1996), 75.

[5]Gregory of Nazianzus, *Oration on Pentecost*, XVI.

[6]Emilio Alvarez, *Pentecostal Orthodoxy: Toward an Ecumenism of the Spirit* (Downers Grove, IL: InterVarsity Press, 2022).

[7]Dale T. Irvin, "Specters of a New Ecumenism: In Search of a Church 'Out of Joint,'" in *Religion, Authority, and the State: Pathways for Ecumenical and Interreligious Dialogue*, ed. L. Lefebure (New York: Palgrave Macmillan, 2016), 1, 17.

[8]Alvarez, *Pentecostal Orthodoxy*.

[9]Stookey, *Calendar*, 75.

[10]Sejin Park, *Pentecost and Sinai: The Festival of Weeks as a Celebration of the Sinai Event* (New York: T&T Clark, 2008), 176.

[11]Park, *Pentecost and Sinai*, 179.

[12]Raymond E. Brown, *A Once and Coming Spirit at Pentecost: Essays on the Liturgical Readings Between Easter and Pentecost, Taken from the Acts of the Apostles and the Gospel According to John* (Collegeville, MN: Liturgical Press, 1994), 10.

3. How Shall We Move?

[1]"Whitsunday," in *The Oxford Dictionary of the Christian Church*, 3rd ed. rev., ed. Frank Leslie Cross and Elizabeth A. Livingstone (New York: Oxford University Press, 2005), 1750.

[2]"Whitsunday," 1750.

[3]Bernard Cook and Gary Macy, *Christian Symbol and Ritual: An Introduction* (New York: Oxford University Press, 2005), 83-84.

[4]Saint Athanasius, *Paschal Letters*, 1379.

[5]"Celebrating the Gift of the Holy Spirit," The Church of England (website), accessed August 13, 2022, www.churchofengland.org/our-faith/what-we-believe/lent-holy-week-and-easter/pentecost.

[6]The Roman Missal (United States Conference of Catholic Bishops, 2011), www.resurrectionparishjohnstown.com/uploads/1/1/4/3

/114314907/theromanmissal.pdf, 75; "Liturgical Color Guide: Understanding the Liturgical Seasons and Colors," Gaspard (website), accessed August 13, 2022, www.gaspardinc.com/liturgical-color-guide.

[7]Father Jeremy, "Green Is Not Just for St Patrick's Day," *Orthodox Road* (blog), June 23, 2013, www.orthodoxroad.com/green-is-not-just-for-st-patricks-day.

[8]Stephen Morris, "Pentecost Greens," Stephen Morris, Author (blog), May 25, 2015, www.stephenmorrisauthor.com/pentecost-greens.

[9]Saint Peter, Bishop of Alexandria, *Syntagma Canonum*, 15.597.

[10]Tertullian, "The Chaplet, or De Corona," in *Ante-Nicene Fathers*, ed. Philip Schaff, Christian Classics Ethereal Library (website), accessed August 21, 2022, www.ccel.org/ccel/schaff/anf03.iv.vi.iii.html.

[11]Peter L'Huillier, *The Church of the Ancient Councils: The Disciplinary Work of the First Four Ecumenical Councils* (Yonkers, NY: St Vladimir's Seminary Press, 2000), 83.

[12]L'Huillier, *Church of the Ancient Councils*, 83.

[13]Saint Basil the Great, *Syntagma Canonum*, 91.528.

[14]Hillsong Young and Free, "To My Knees," *Youth Revival* (Brentwood, TN: Sparrow Records, 2016).

[15]"Prayer," *Encyclopedia of Early Christianity*, 2nd ed., ed. Everett Ferguson (New York: Garland, 1998), 938.

[16]"Proskynēsis," Oxford Reference, www.oxfordreference.com/view/10.1093/oi/authority.20110803100350210.

4. Pentecost Prayers, Hymns, and Scriptures

[1]"Saint Symeon's Hymn #25, with Thanks to Tim," Monasteries of the Heart (website), posted June 2, 2016, www.monasteriesoftheheart.org/st-symeon-new-theologian-prayer-heart/saint-symeon%27s-hymn-25-thanks-tim. This version of Symeon's hymn is a modified free-verse translation by Father George Maloney.

[2]"Sunday of Holy Pentecost," Greek Orthodox Archdiocese of America (website), copyright 2021, www.goarch.org/pentecost.

[3]Editors of Encyclopedia, "kontakion," *Britannica*, July 20, 1998, www
.britannica.com/art/kontakion.

[4]"Sunday of Holy Pentecost," www.goarch.org/pentecost.

[5]"Sunday of Holy Pentecost," www.goarch.org/pentecost.

[6]"Kneeling Prayers of Pentecost," Holy Trinity Greek Orthodox Church
(website), June 24, 2019, htrinityportland.org/2019/06/24/kneeling
-prayers-of-pentecost.

[7]For those interested in the subject see: Michael J. Christensen and
Jeffrey A. Wittung, *Partakers of the Divine Nature: The History and
Development of Deification in the Christian Traditions* (Grand Rapids,
MI: Baker Books, 2007).

[8]Peter G. Cobb, "The History of the Christian Year," *The Study of
Liturgy*, ed. Cheslyn Jones et al., rev. ed. (New York: Oxford University Press, 1992), 464.

[9]The Roman Missal (United States Conference of Catholic Bishops,
2011), www.resurrectionparishjohnstown.com/uploads/1/1/4/3
/114314907/theromanmissal.pdf, 447.

[10]St. Augustine, *Confessions*, trans. Henry Chadwick (New York:
Oxford University Press, 1991).

[11]Frank X. Blisard, "The Seven Gifts of the Holy Spirit," Catholic Answers (website), June 10, 2019, www.catholic.com/magazine/print-
edition/the-seven-gifts-of-the-holy-spirit.

[12]Editors of Encyclopedia, "God the Father," *Britannica*, updated June
9, 2022, www.britannica.com/topic/Christianity/God-the-Father.

[13]Robert J. Glendinning, *Early Christianity in Its Song and Verse: CE
300-1300* (Pembina, ND: FriesenPress, 2015), 205.

[14]"The Lessons Appointed for Use on the Day of Pentecost," The Lectionary Page (website), accessed August 21, 2022, www.lectionarypage
.net/YearC/Pentecost/CPentDay.html.

[15]"Readings for the Vigil of Pentecost," The Liturgy Archive (website), accessed August 20, 2022, www.liturgies.net/Liturgies/Catholic/roman
_missal/readings/pentecostvigil#gospel1.

[16]Roman Missal, 1436.

[17]Roman Missal, 448.

[18]"Canticle: The Song of the Three Holy Children," A Collection of Prayers (website), accessed August 21, 2022, acollectionofprayers.com /2017/05/16/canticle-the-song-of-the-three-holy-children.

[19]Roman Missal, 448.

[20]Tertullian, *A Treatise on the Soul* (Boston: Wyatt North Publishing, LLC, 2020).

[21]Gregory of Nyssa, *On the Origin of Man*, Gnos 44.

[22]Basil the Great, *Exegetic Homilies on the Psalms*, 19.8.

[23]Roman Missal, 449.

[24]Roman Missal, 449.

[25]Roman Missal, 449.

[26]Roman Missal, 449.

[27]Glendinning, *Early Christianity in Its Song*, 149-50.

[28]"Prayer for the Seven Gifts of the Holy Spirit," Our Catholic Prayers (website), accessed August 22, 2022, www.ourcatholicprayers.com /prayer-for-the-seven-gifts-of-the-holy-spirit.html.

[29]*The Malankara Orthodox Syrian Christian's Holy Liturgy of Pentecosti* (Mississauga, ON: St. Gregorios Indian Orthodox Church, 2013), www.stthomasokc.com/concept/activities/Pentecost_Service.pdf, 5.

[30]For more information on the Pentecost liturgy in the Syrian Orthodox tradition, see Baby Varghese, *Western Syrian Liturgical Theology: Liturgy, Worship and Society* (London: Routledge, 2004).

[31]Eniyono means "responsaria." The congregation responds or gives answer to the priests or deacons. "Liturgical Music," The Malankara Orthodox Syrian Church (website), copyright 2015, mosc.in/the_church /liturgy/liturgical-music.

[32]"Meaning of Syriac and Greek Words," St. Gregorios Malankara Orthodox Cathedral (website), accessed August 22, 2022, stgregorioscathedral .com/orthodox-terminology.

[33]*Malankara Orthodox Syrian Christian's Holy Liturgy*, 12.

[34]*Malankara Orthodox Syrian Christian's Holy Liturgy*, 24-25.

[35]*Malankara Orthodox Syrian Christian's Holy Liturgy*, 38.

[36]The Order of Confirmation," 1928 Book of Common Prayer, http://episcopalnet.org/1928bcp/confirmation.html.

[37]*Gregory of Nyssa: The Life of Moses*, trans. Abraham Malherbe and Everett Ferguson, Classics of Western Spirituality series (New York: Paulist Press, 1978), 83.

[38]Hilary of Poitiers (attributed), trans. Robert Campbell, "Hail This Joyful Day's Return," in *Hymns and Songs of Praise for Public and Social Worship*, ed. Roswell D. Hitchcock, Zachary Eddy, and Philip Schaff (New York: A. S. Barnes, 1874), https://hymnary.org/hymn/HSPP1874/371.

[39]James K. A. Smith, *Thinking in Tongues: Pentecostal Contributions to Christian Philosophy* (Grand Rapids, MI: Eerdmans, 2010), xvi.

[40]Teresa L. Reed, "Shared Possessions: Black Pentecostals, Afro-Caribbeans, and Sacred Music," *Black Music Research Journal* 32, No. 1 (Spring 2012): 5-25.

[41]Melvin L. Butler, "In Zora's Footsteps: Experiencing Music and Pentecostal Ritual in the African Diaspora," *Obsidian* 9, No. 1 (Spring/Summer 2008): 74-106.

The Fullness of Time Series

Each volume in the Fullness of Time series invites readers to engage with the riches of the church year, exploring the traditions, prayers, Scriptures, and rituals of the seasons of the church calendar.

LENT
Esau McCaulley

ADVENT
Tish Harrison Warren

EASTER
Wesley Hill

CHRISTMAS
Emily McGowin

PENTECOST
Emilio Alvarez

EPIPHANY
Fleming Rutledge